Be Complete

Warren W. Wiersbe

This book is designed for your personal reading pleasure and profit. It is also designed for group study. A leader's guide with helps and hints for teachers and visual aids (Victor Multiuse Transparency Masters) is available from your local bookstore or from the publisher.

VICTOR

BOOKS a division of SP Publications, Inc.
WHEATON. ILLINOIS 60187

Offices also in
Whitby, Ontario, Canada
Amersham-on-the-Hill, Bucks, England

BE Books by Warren Wiersbe

Be Loyal *(Matthew)*	Be Complete *(Colossians)*
Be Right *(Romans)*	Be Ready *(1 & 2 Thessalonians)*
Be Wise *(1 Corinthians)*	Be Faithful *(1 & 2 Timothy, Titus)*
Be Encouraged *(2 Corinthians)*	Be Confident *(Hebrews)*
Be Free *(Galatians)*	Be Mature *(James)*
Be Rich *(Ephesians)*	Be Hopeful *(1 Peter)*
Be Joyful *(Philippians)*	Be Alert *(2 Peter, 2 & 3 John, Jude)*

Be Real *(1 John)*

Seventh printing, 1984

Recommended Dewey Decimal Classification: 227.7
Suggested Subject Headings: BIBLE, N.T. COLOSSIANS

Library of Congress Catalog Card Number: 80-52901
ISBN: 0-89693-726-7

VICTOR BOOKS
A division of SP Publications, Inc.
Wheaton, Illinois 60187

CONTENTS

*Dedicated to some Florida friends
who have enriched and enlarged
my life and ministry:*

*Mrs. Jessie Byerly
Bill and Marge Caldwell
Joe and Melva Hanscom
Mrs. Antoinette McFadden*

PREFACE

I began this study of Colossians with much fear and trembling, for it is one of the most profound letters Paul ever wrote. Now that I have completed these chapters, I realize even more the depths of spiritual truth found in Colossians.

The message of this letter is greatly needed today. I hear too many voices telling me that I need something more than Jesus Christ—some exciting experience, some new doctrine, some addition to my Christian experience. But Paul affirms that what I need is *appropriation of what I already have in Christ.* "And ye are complete in Him."

I also hear voices that want to judge me and rob me of the glorious liberty I have in Christ. How encouraging to hear Paul say: "Let no man beguile you, let no man spoil you, let no man judge you." The fullness of Christ is all that I need, and all man-made regulations and disciplines cannot replace the riches I have in God's Son.

These few chapters cannot begin to mine all of the treasures that are in this letter. But if these simple studies introduce you to your fullness in Christ, and encourage you to appropriate them, then I will be grateful to the Lord. I have a feeling that we would have revival in our churches if all true believers dared to live what Colossians teaches.

WARREN W. WIERSBE

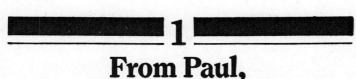

1

From Paul, with Love

Colossians 1:1-2

Do the heavenly bodies have any influence over our lives? The millions of people who consult their horoscopes each day would say, "Yes!" In the United States, there are about 1750 daily newspapers, and 1220 of them carry astrological data!

• Is there any relationship between diet and spiritual living?

• Does God speak to us immediately, in our minds, or only through His Word, the Bible?

• Do the Eastern religions have something to offer the evangelical Christian?

These questions sound very contemporary. Yet they are the very issues Paul dealt with in his magnificent Epistle to the Colossians. We need this important letter today just as they needed it back in A.D. 60 when Paul wrote it.

The City
Colossae was one of three cities located about 100 miles inland from Ephesus. The other two cities were Laodicea and Hierapolis (Col. 4:13, 16).

7

This area was a meeting point of East and West because an important trade route passed through there. At one time, all three cities were growing and prosperous, but gradually Colossae slipped into a second-rate position. It became what we would call a small town. Yet the church there was important enough to merit the attention of the Apostle Paul.

All kinds of philosophies mingled in this cosmopolitan area, and religious hucksters abounded. There was a large Jewish colony in Colossae, and there was also a constant influx of new ideas and doctrines from the East. It was fertile ground for religious speculations and heresies!

The Church

Colossae probably would never have been mentioned in the New Testament had it not been for the church there. The city is never named in the Book of Acts because Paul did not start the Colossian church nor did he ever visit it. Paul had *heard* of their faith (Col. 1:4, 9); but he had never seen these believers personally (2:1). Here was a church of unknown people, in a small town, receiving an inspired letter from the great Apostle Paul!

How did the Colossian church begin? It was the outgrowth of Paul's three-year ministry in Ephesus (Acts 19; 20:17-38). So effective was the witness of the church at Ephesus that "all they which dwelt in Asia heard the word of the Lord Jesus, both Jews and Greeks" (Acts 19:10). This would include people in Colossae, Laodicea, and Hierapolis.

When we examine the persons involved in the prison correspondence of Paul (see Eph., Phil., Col., Phile., and 2 Tim.), we can just about put the story together of how the Colossian church was founded. During Paul's ministry in Ephesus, at least two men from Colossae were brought to faith in Jesus Christ—Epaphras and Philemon (see Phile. 19). Epaphras apparently was one of the key founders of the church in Colossae, for he shared the Gospel with his friends there (Col. 1:7). He also had a ministry in the cities of Hierapolis and Laodicea (Col. 4:12-13).

Philemon had a church meeting in his home (Phile. 2). It is likely that Apphia and Archippus, mentioned in this verse, were respectively the wife and son of Philemon, and that Archippus was the pastor of the church (Col. 4:17).

There is a good lesson for us here: God does not always need an apostle, or a "full-time Christian worker" to get a ministry established. Nor does He need elaborate buildings and extensive organizations. Here were two laymen who were used of God to start ministries in at least three cities. It is God's plan that the Christians in the large urban areas, like Ephesus, reach out into the smaller towns and share the Gospel. Is *your* church helping to evangelize "small-town" mission fields?

The Colossian assembly was predominantly Gentile in its membership. The sins that Paul named (Col. 3:5-9) were commonly associated with the Gentiles, and his statement about the mystery applied more to the Gentiles than to the Jews (1:25-29). The church was probably about five years old when Paul wrote this letter.

The Crisis

Why did Paul write this letter to the church in Colossae? Because a crisis had occurred that was about to destroy the ministry of the church. By comparing the prison letters, we can arrive at the following reconstruction of events.

Paul was at that time a prisoner in Rome (Acts 21:17—28:31). He met a runaway slave named Onesimus, who belonged to Philemon, one of the leaders of the church in Colossae. Paul led Onesimus to Christ. He then wrote his letter to Philemon, asking his friend to forgive Onesimus and receive him back as a brother in Christ.

About the same time, Epaphras showed up in Rome because he needed Paul's help. Some new doctrines were being taught in Colossae and were invading the church and creating problems. So Paul wrote this letter to the Colossians in order to refute these heretical teachings and establish the truth of the Gospel.

Epaphras remained with Paul in Rome (Col. 4:12-13). Onesimus and Tychicus carried Paul's epistles to their destinations: Ephesians 6:21, Colossians 4:7-9; and Philemon. Epaphras was called Paul's "fellow-prisoner," a title also given to Aristarchus (Phile. 23; Col. 4:10). This suggests that Epaphras *willingly* remained with Paul to assist him. Neither Aristarchus nor Epaphras was a prisoner because he broke the law and was arrested. They were Paul's willing companions, sacrificing their own comfort to help him.

What was the heresy that threatened the peace and purity of the Colossian church? It was a combination of Eastern philosophy and Jewish legalism, with elements of what Bible scholars call Gnosticism (NOS-ti-cism). This term comes from the Greek word *gnosis* (KNOW-sis) which means "to know." (An *agnostic* is one who does not know.) The Gnostics were the people who were "in the know" when it came to the deep things of God. They were the "spiritual aristocracy" in the church.

To begin with, this heresy promised people such a close union with God that they would achieve a "spiritual perfection." Spiritual fullness could be theirs only if they entered into the teachings and ceremonies prescribed. There was also a "full knowledge," a spiritual depth, that only the initiated could enjoy. This "wisdom" would release them from earthly things and put them in touch with heavenly things.

Of course, all of this teaching was but man-made philosophy based on traditions and not on divine truth (Col. 2:8). It grew out of the philosophical question, *Why is there evil in this world if creation was made by a holy God?* As these philosophers speculated and pondered, they came to the false conclusion that matter was evil. Their next false conclusion was that a holy God could not come into contact with evil matter, so there had to be a series of "emanations" from God to His creation. They believed in a powerful spirit world that used material things to attack mankind. They also held to a form of astrology, believing that angelic beings ruled heavenly bodies and influenced affairs on earth. (See Col. 1:16; 2:10, 15.)

Added to these Eastern speculations was a form of Jewish legalism. The teachers believed that the rite of circumcision was helpful in spiritual development (Col. 2:11). They taught that the Old Testament Law, especially the dietary laws, were also useful in attaining spiritual perfection (2:14-17). Definite rules and regulations told them what was evil and what was good (2:21).

Since to them matter was evil, they had to find some way to control their own human natures in this pursuit of perfection. Two different practices resulted. One school of thought held that the only way to conquer evil matter was by means of rigid discipline and asceticism (2:23). The other view taught that it was permissible to engage in all kinds of sin, since matter was evil anyway! It appears that the first opinion was the predominant one in Colossae.

It is easy to see how this kind of teaching undermined the very foundations of the Christian faith. To begin with, these heretics attacked the Person and work of Jesus Christ. To them, He was merely one of God's many "emanations" and not the very Son of God, come in the flesh. The Incarnation means *God with us* (Matt. 1:23), but these false teachers claimed that God was keeping His distance from us! When we trust the Son of God, there is no need for intermediary beings between us and heaven!

In His work on the cross, Jesus Christ settled the sin question (Col. 1:20) and completely defeated all satanic forces (2:15). He put an end to the legal demands of the Law (2:14-17). In fact, Jesus Christ alone is the Preeminent One! (1:18; 3:11) All that the believer needs is Jesus!

Matter is not evil, and the human body is not evil. Each person is born with a fallen human nature that wants to control the body and use it for sin; but the body itself is not evil. If that were the case, Jesus Christ would never have come to earth in a human body. Nor would He have enjoyed the everyday blessings of life as He ministered on earth, such as attending wedding feasts and accepting invitations to dinner. Diets and disciplines can be good for one's health, but they have no power to develop true spirituality (2:20-23).

As for astrology and the influence of angels and heavenly bodies, Paul denounced this with vigor.

On the cross, Jesus won a complete victory over all satanic powers (2:15). Christians do not need to turn to the rudiments of the world (2:8, 20). This word translated *rudiments* means "elemental beings" or "elementary principles." In this case, it refers to the beings that (according to the Gnostics) controlled the heavenly bodies that in turn controlled events on earth. Believers who consult horoscopes substitute superstition for revelation and deny the Person and work of Christ.

This false teaching was a deceptive combination of many things: Jewish legalism, Oriental philosophy, pagan astrology, mysticism, asceticism, and even a touch of Christianity. There was something for everybody, and this was what made it so dangerous. The false teachers claimed that they were not *denying* the Christian faith, but only lifting it to a higher level. They offered fullness and freedom, a satisfying life that solved all the problems that people face.

Do we have any of this heresy today? Yes, we do; and it is just as deceptive and dangerous! When we make Jesus Christ and the Christian revelation only *part* of a total religious system or philosophy, we cease to give Him the preeminence. When we strive for "spiritual perfection" or "spiritual fullness" by means of formulas, disciplines, or rituals, we go backward instead of forward. Christian believers must beware of mixing their Christian faith with such alluring things as yoga, transcendental meditation, Oriental mysticism, and the like. We must also beware of "deeper life" teachers who offer a system for victory and fullness that bypasses devotion to Jesus Christ. In all things, He must have the preeminence!

This heresy was in direct contrast to the teaching

of Paul. It took a negative view of life: "God is far away, matter is evil, and demonic forces are constantly threatening us." The Christian faith teaches that God is near us, that God made all things good (although they can be used for evil), and that Christ has delivered His people from the powers of darkness (Col. 1:13). This heresy turned the world into a frightful prison, while Jesus made it clear that the Father is at work in this world caring for His own. Finally, these false teachers tried to change people from the outside, by means of diets and disciplines. But true spiritual growth comes from within.

The Correspondence

With this background, we can now look at Paul's letter to the Colossians and get an overview of what he has written. We know that his epistle to the Ephesians was written and sent about the same time as his Colossian letter. Keeping this in mind, we can discover many parallels between these two letters. However, the emphasis in Ephesians is on the church, the body of Christ; but the emphasis in Colossians is on Christ, the Head of the body.

In this letter, Paul used the vocabulary of the false teachers, but he did not use their definitions. He used these words in their true Christian meaning. As we study Colossians, we will find words such as *fullness, perfect, complete,* all of which were used by the Gnostic heretics. Over 30 times Paul used the little word *all.* He also wrote about *wisdom* which was a key term in the Gnostic vocabulary; he had a great deal to say about angels and spirit powers too.

His main theme was *the preeminence of Jesus Christ* (Col. 1:18; 3:11). There is no need for us to

worry about angelic mediators or spiritual emanations. God has sent His Son to die for us! Every
person who believes on Jesus Christ is saved and
is a part of His body, the church, of which He is
the Head (1:18). We are united to Christ in a
wonderful living relationship!

Furthermore, nothing need be added to this relationship, because each believer is "complete in
Him" (2:10). All of God's fullness dwells in Christ
(2:9), and we share that fullness! "For in Christ
all the fullness of the Deity lives in bodily form,
and you have been given fullness in Christ" (2:9-
10a, NIV).

While in an airport waiting for my plane to be
called, I was approached by a young man who
wanted to sell me a book. One look at the garish
cover told me that the book was filled with Oriental
myths and philosophies.

"I have a book here that meets all my needs," I
told the young man, and I reached into my brief-
case and took out my Bible.

"Oh, we aren't against the Bible!" he assured me.
"It's just that we have something more, and it makes
our faith even better."

"Nobody can give me more than Jesus Christ has
already given me," I replied. I turned to Colossians
2, but by that time the young man was hurrying
down the corridor.

Sad to say, there are many Christians who
actually believe that some person, religious system,
or discipline can add something to their spiritual
experience. But they already have everything they
ever will need in the Person and work of Jesus
Christ.

If Paul had made an outline of his letter to the
Colossian Christians, it might look like this:

Theme: Jesus Christ is Preeminent (1:18)

I. **DOCTRINE: CHRIST'S PREEMINENCE DECLARED—CHAPTER 1**
   1. In the Gospel message—1:1-12
   2. In redemption—1:13-14
   3. In Creation—1:15-17
   4. In the church—1:18-23
   5. In Paul's ministry—1:24-29
II. **DANGER: CHRIST'S PREEMINENCE DEFENDED—CHAPTER 2**
   1. Beware of empty philosophies—2:1-10
   2. Beware of religious legalism—2:11-17
   3. Beware of man-made disciplines—2:18-23
III. **DUTY: CHRIST'S PREEMINENCE DEMONSTRATED—CHAPTERS 3—4**
   1. In personal purity—3:1-11
   2. In Christian fellowship—3:12-17
   3. In the home—3:18-21
   4. In daily work—3:22—4:1
   5. In Christian witness—4:2-6
   6. In Christian service—4:7-18

This is, of course, only a *suggested* outline and must not be construed as being inspired. There are many ways in which the Word of God may be analyzed and outlined, and no outline must ever take the place of the written Word itself.

As we study this outline, however, we see how Paul approached this problem and tried to solve it. He did not begin by attacking the false teachers and their doctrines. He began by exalting Jesus Christ and showing His preeminence in five areas: the Gospel message, redemption, Creation, the church, and Paul's own ministry. The people to whom Paul was writing had become Christians because of the Gospel message brought to them by Epaphras. If this message was wrong, then they were not saved at all!

Once he had established the preeminence of Christ, then Paul attacked the heretics on their own ground. In chapter 2, Paul exposed the false origin of their teachings and showed how their teachings contradicted everything Paul taught about Jesus Christ. The believer who masters this chapter is not likely to be led astray by some alluring and enticing "new-and-improved brand of Christianity."

But Paul did not think his task completed when he had refuted the heretics, for he still had some important words for the church. In chapters 3 and 4, Paul explained the greatest antidote to false teaching—*a godly life*. Those who say, "I don't care what you believe, just so long as you live a good life" are not thinking logically. *What we believe determines how we behave.* If we believe that matter is evil, we will use our bodies one way; but if we believe that our bodies are temples of the Holy Spirit, we will live accordingly.

Wrong doctrine always leads to wrong living. Right doctrine should lead to right living. In the two concluding chapters, Paul applied the preeminence of Christ to the daily affairs of life. If Christ is truly preeminent in our lives, then we will glorify Him by keeping pure, by enjoying fellowship with other saints, by loving each other at home and being faithful at work, and by seeking to witness for Christ and serve Him effectively. Unless doctrine leads to duty, it is of no use to us.

Many Bible scholars have concluded that Colossians is the most profound letter Paul ever wrote. This must not keep us from reading and studying this wonderful letter. But we must be cautioned against a superficial approach to these chapters. Unless we depend on the Spirit of God to teach us, we will miss the truths God wants us to learn.

The church today desperately needs the message of Colossians. We live in a day when religious toleration is interpreted to mean "one religion is just as good as another." Some people try to take the best from various religious systems and manufacture their own private religion. To many people, Jesus Christ is only *one* of several great religious teachers, with no more authority than they. He may be prominent, but He is definitely not preeminent.

This is an age of "syncretism." People are trying to harmonize and unite many different schools of thought and come up with a superior religion. Our evangelical churches are in danger of diluting the faith in their loving attempt to understand the beliefs of others. Mysticism, legalism, Eastern religions, asceticism, and man-made philosophies are secretly creeping into churches. They are not denying Christ, but they are dethroning Him and robbing Him of His rightful place of preeminence.

As we study this exciting letter, we must heed Paul's warnings: "Lest any man should beguile you" (2:4), "Lest any man spoil you" (2:8), "Let no man therefore judge you!" (2:16)

2
Miracles
at Colossae

Colossians 1:3-8

The famous Scottish preacher, Alexander Whyte, was known as an appreciator. He loved to write postcards to people, thanking them for some kindness or blessing they had brought to his life. Those messages often brought a touch of encouragement to a heart just when it was needed most. Appreciation is great medicine for the soul.

The Apostle Paul was a great encourager, and this epistle is a good example of the grace of thanksgiving. In this section (which is one long sentence in the original Greek), he gives thanks for what Christ has done in the lives of the Colossian Christians. But he also mentions thanksgiving in five other places in this letter: 1:12; 2:7; 3:15 and 17; and 4:2. When you recall that Paul wrote this letter *in prison,* his attitude of thanksgiving is even more wonderful.

Like Paul, we should be grateful for what God is doing in the lives of others. As Christians, we are all members of one body (1 Cor. 12:12-13). If one member of the body is strengthened, this helps to strengthen the entire body. If one church experiences a revival touch from God, it will help all the churches. In this expression of thanksgiving, Paul traced the stages in the spiritual experience of the Colossian believers.

They Heard the Gospel (Col. 1:5b-7)

The good news of the Gospel was not native to their city. It had to be brought to them; and in their case, Epaphras was the messenger. He was himself a citizen of Colossae (4:12-13), but he had come in contact with Paul and had been converted to Jesus Christ. This was probably during Paul's great three-year ministry in Ephesus (Acts 19:10).

Once Epaphras had been saved, he shared this thrilling news with his relatives and friends back home. Perhaps it would have been exciting for Epaphras to stay with Paul in Ephesus where so many wonderful things were taking place. But his first responsibility was to take the Gospel to his own home city. (See Mark 5:19.)

The Gospel is the good news that Jesus Christ has solved the problem of sin through His death, burial, and resurrection. The word *Gospel* means "good news." Unfortunately, some people witness as though the Gospel is the bad news of condemnation.

I recall one church officer who was more of a prosecuting attorney than a Christian witness. Though he constantly reproved people for their sins, he failed to share the good news of forgiveness through faith in Christ.

But we can learn a lesson from him. In our witnessing, we should remember to emphasize the good news of the Gospel. (See 1 Cor. 15:1-8.) In this section in his letter to the Colossians, Paul reviews the characteristics of this exciting Gospel message.

It centers in a Person—Jesus Christ. The theme of this epistle is the preeminence of Jesus Christ, and He is certainly preeminent in the Gospel. The false teachers who had invaded the fellowship in Colossae were trying to remove Jesus Christ from His place of preeminence; but to do this was to destroy the Gospel. It is *Christ* who died for us, and who arose again. The Gospel message does not center in a philosophy, a doctrine, or a religious system. It centers in Jesus Christ, the Son of God.

It is the "word of truth" (1:5, NIV). This means that it came from God and can be trusted. "Thy Word is truth" (John 17:17). There are many messages and ideas that can be called *true,* but only God's Word can be called *truth.* Satan is the liar; to believe his lies is to be led astray into death (John 8:44). Jesus is the Truth (John 14:6); when we trust Him, we experience life. Men have tried to destroy God's truth, but they have failed. The Word of truth still stands!

Everybody has faith in something. But faith is only as good as the object in which a person puts his trust. The jungle pagan worships a god of stone; the educated city pagan worships money or possessions or status. In both cases, faith is empty. The true Christian believer has faith in Jesus Christ, and that faith is based on the Word of truth. Any other kind of faith is but superstition—it cannot save.

It is the message of God's grace (1:6b). Two words in the Christian vocabulary are often confused: *grace* and *mercy.* God in His grace gives me what I do not deserve. Yet God in His mercy does not give me what I do deserve. Grace is God's favor shown to undeserving sinners. The reason the

Gospel is *good* news is because of grace: God is
willing and able to save all who will trust Jesus
Christ.

John Selden (1584-1654) was a leading historian
and legal authority in England. He had a library
of 8000 volumes and was recognized for his learning. When he was dying, he said to Archbishop
Ussher: "I have surveyed most of the learning that
is among the sons of men, and my study is filled
with books and manuscripts on various subjects.
But at present, I cannot recollect any passage out
of all my books and papers whereon I can rest my
soul, save this from the sacred Scriptures: 'The
grace of God that bringeth salvation hath appeared
to all men' (Titus 2:11)."

It is for the whole world (1:6). When I was a
young pastor, one of my favorite preachers was
Dr. Walter Wilson of Kansas City. He had a unique
way of making old truths seem new and exciting.
I once heard him quote John 3:16 and ask, "If you
were to give a gift that would be suitable for the
whole world, what would you give?"

He then listed several possibilities and showed
how those gifts could not suit everybody: books
(many people cannot read); foods (people eat
different things in different parts of the world);
clothing (climates are different); money (not every
culture makes use of money). He came to the
logical conclusion that only the Gospel, with its
gift of eternal life, was suitable for the whole world;
and he was right.

Paul said that the Gospel was bearing fruit in all
the world. The Word of God is the only seed that
can be planted anywhere in the world, and it will
bear fruit. The Gospel can be preached "to every
creature which is under heaven" (Col. 1:23). Paul's

emphasis was on "every man" (1:28). False teachers do not take their message to all the world. They go where the Gospel has already gone and try to lead believers astray. *They have no good news for lost sinners!*

If people are to be saved, they must hear the Gospel of Jesus Christ. And if they are to hear, we who are saved must carry the message. Are you doing your part?

They Believed in Jesus Christ (Col. 1:4)

It is possible to hear and not believe, even though the Word of God has the power to generate faith in those who hear (Rom. 10:17). Millions of people have heard the good news of salvation and yet not believed. But those who believe in Jesus Christ receive from God the gift of eternal life (John 3:14-18).

We are not saved by faith *in faith*. There is a cult of "believism" today that promotes faith but has little to do with Jesus Christ. Even some popular songs carry the message of faith in faith. The modern attitude is, "If you believe, you are safe." But the obvious question is, "Believe in *what?*" The answer: "Just believe!"

Nor are we saved by faith *in a set of doctrines.* I have often told the story about the famous evangelist, George Whitefield, who was witnessing to a man. "What do you believe?" Whitefield asked. The man replied, "I believe what my church believes."

"And what does your church believe?" asked the evangelist.

"What I believe," replied the man.

Undaunted, Whitefield tried again and asked,

"And what do you *both* believe?"

"Why, we both believe the same thing!" was the man's evasive reply.

Saving faith involves the mind, the emotions, and the will. With the mind we understand the truth of the Gospel, and with the heart we feel conviction and the need to be saved. But it is only when we exercise the will and commit ourselves to Christ that the process is complete. Faith is not mental assent to a body of doctrines, no matter how true those doctrines may be. Faith is not emotional concern. *Faith is commitment to Jesus Christ.*

When missionary John G. Paton was translating the Bible in the Outer Hebrides, he searched for the exact word to translate *believe*. Finally, he discovered it: the word meant "lean your whole weight upon." That is what saving faith is—leaning your whole weight upon Jesus Christ.

Saving faith is grounded in the Gospel (Col. 1:23). It is the Word of God that gives us assurance. As we grow in the Lord, our faith becomes steadfast (2:5) and established (2:7).

The false teachers who had come to Colossae tried to undermine the saints' faith in Christ and the Word. This same kind of undermining goes on today. Any religious teaching that dethrones Jesus Christ, or that makes salvation other than an experience of God's grace through faith, is anti-Christian and born of Satan.

One final thought: the experience of the believers in Colossae was so wonderful that people talked about it! Paul heard about it from Epaphras; the false teachers heard about it and decided to visit the Colossian assembly to see the remarkable change for themselves.

You cannot keep silent once you have experienced salvation in Jesus Christ. Is your Christian life the kind that encourages others and makes it easy for them to witness? Is your church fellowship so exciting that even the unsaved are taking notice?

They Were Discipled (Col. 1:7)

Epaphras did not simply lead the Colossians to Christ and then abandon them. He taught them the Word and sought to establish their faith. The word translated "learned" in verse 7 is related to the word *disciple* in the Greek language. It is the same word Jesus used: "Learn of Me" (Matt. 11:29) or, in effect, "Become My disciple."

These new believers were in danger of turning from the truth and following the false teachers. Paul reminded them that it was Epaphras who led them to Christ, discipled them, and taught them the Word. The word *before* (Col. 1:5) probably means "before these false teachers appeared on the scene." Like the Colossians, we should beware of any religious leader who does not seek to win lost souls, but who devotes himself to "stealing sheep" from the flocks of others.

We should never forget that new Christians must be discipled. Just as the newborn baby needs loving care and protection till he can care for himself, so the new Christian needs discipling. The Great Commission does not stop with the salvation of the lost, for in that commission Jesus commanded us to teach converts the Word as well (Matt. 28:19-20). That is what the fellowship of the local church is all about. The New Testament does not teach the kind of "individual Christianity" that is so prevalent today—people who ignore the local church and who find all their spiritual food in books, radio, TV, or cassette tapes.

Epaphras was a faithful minister. He not only won people to Christ, but he taught them the Word and helped them to grow. He also prayed for them (Col. 4:12-13) that they might become mature in Jesus Christ. When danger threatened the members of the church, Epaphras went to Rome to get counsel from Paul. He loved his people and wanted to protect them from false doctrines that would destroy the fellowship and hinder their spiritual development.

The word *disciple* is found more than 260 times in the Gospels and Acts, and the verb translated, "to learn as a disciple" is found 25 times in the New Testament. In that day, a disciple was not simply a person who sat and listened to a teacher. He was someone who lived with the teacher and who learned by listening, looking, and living. Discipleship involved more than enrolling in a school and attending lectures. It meant total surrender to the teacher. It meant learning by living. Perhaps our modern day medical students or trade apprentices come close to illustrating the meaning of discipleship.

But we who disciple other believers must be careful not to get in the way. We are not to make disciples *for ourselves,* but for Jesus Christ. We must relate people to Him so that they love and obey Him. Epaphras faithfully taught his people and related them to Jesus Christ, but the false teachers came in and tried to "draw away disciples." (Dr. Luke warns about this problem. See Acts 20:28-30.) Human nature has the tendency to want to follow men instead of God—to want "something new" instead of the basic foundational truths of the Gospel.

Now we come to the results of Epaphras' efforts.

They Became Faithful in Christ (Col. 1:6, 8)

The Word of God is seed (Luke 8:11). This means the Word has life in it (Heb. 4:12). When it is planted in the heart, it can produce fruit. "All over the world this Gospel is producing fruit and growing" (Col. 1:6, NIV).

Near King's Cross station in London, England, there is a cemetery containing a unique grave, that of the agnostic Lady Ann Grimston. She is buried in a marble tomb, marked by a marble slab. Before she died, she said sarcastically to a friend, "I shall live again as surely as a tree will grow from my body."

An unbeliever, Lady Ann Grimston did not believe that there was life after death. However, *a tree did grow from her grave!* A tiny seed took root, and as it grew, it cracked the marble and even tore the metal railing out of the ground! There is life and power in a seed, and there is life and power in the Word of God.

When God's Word is planted and cultivated, it produces fruit. Faith, hope, and love are among the firstfruits in the spiritual harvest. These spiritual graces are among the evidences that a person has truly been born again. (See 1 Thes. 1:3; Rom. 5:1-4; Heb. 6:9-12; Eph. 1:13-15; 1 Peter 1:3-9.)

Faith comes through the hearing of God's Word (Rom. 10:17). Our Christian lives start with *saving* faith; but this is only the beginning. We learn to walk by faith (2 Cor. 5:7) and work by faith (1 Thes. 1:3). It is faith that gives power to prayer (Luke 17:5-6). Faith is a shield that protects us from Satan's fiery darts (Eph. 6:16).

Love is another evidence of true salvation, for the unsaved person is wrapped up mainly in himself (Eph. 2:1-3). The fact that these people loved *all* the saints was proof that God had changed them and given them eternal life. Christian love is not a shallow feeling that we manufacture; it is the work of the Holy Spirit in our hearts (Col. 1:8; Rom. 5:5). It is worth noting that Colossians 1:8 is the only verse in the letter that mentions the Holy Spirit, and it is in connection with love.

This Spirit-given love was for "all the saints" (1:4) and not only for the people of their own fellowship. As Christians, we also need to realize the vastness of God's love and share it with all the saints (Eph. 3:17-19). Believers should be "knit together in love" (Col. 2:2) so that there will be a true spiritual unity to the glory of God. The bond that unites us is love (Col. 3:14). Uniformity is the result of compulsion from the outside; unity is the result of compassion on the inside.

Hope is also a characteristic of the believer. Unsaved people are without hope because they are without God (Eph. 2:11-12). Those outside of Christ have no hope (1 Thes. 4:13). In the Bible, *hope* does not mean "hope so." Our hope in Christ is as definite and assured as our faith in Christ. Because Christ is in us, we have the "hope of glory" (Col. 1:27).

The false teachers tried to unsettle the Colossian believers and move them away from the hope of the Gospel (1:23). But Paul made it clear that this hope is "laid up" for believers in heaven (1:5). The word translated *laid up* carries the meaning of "to be reserved, to be set aside for someone." It was used to refer to money laid up or hidden. The tense of the verb indicates that this hope has *once and for all* been reserved so that nothing can take it from us. Not only has this hope (our glorious inheritance in glory) been reserved for us, but we are being kept by God's power so that we can be sure of enjoying heaven one day! (1 Peter 1:1-5) We are being guarded for glory!

What is the relationship between faith, hope, and love? Certainly the more we love someone, the more we will trust him. We do not trust a casual acquaintance to the same degree that we trust a confidential friend. As we come to know God better, we trust Him more and we love Him more. Love and faith encourage each other.

But hope also has a valuable contribution to make. Wherever there is a relationship of faith and love, there will be a growing hope. When a man and woman fall in love and learn to trust each other in that love, their future always becomes brighter. In fact, Paul taught that hope is a motivating power for love and for faith: ". . . the faith and love that spring from the hope that is stored up for you in heaven" (Col. 1:5, NIV).

The blessed hope of seeing Jesus Christ and going to heaven to be with Him is a powerful force in the Christian's life. When we realize the joy we shall have in heaven, it makes us love Him more. The fact that we *know* we shall be with Him in glory encourages us to trust Him more. Even the problems and trials here on earth do not move us away from that hope.

I have noticed that the prospect of a future happiness has a way of making people love one another more. Have you ever watched children just before Christmas or a family vacation? The bright promise of heaven encourages our faith and expands our love. Then faith and love work together to make the present more enjoyable and the future more exciting.

Divisions and dissensions among Christians are tragic. I am not suggesting that we all get together in a "super church," but I do feel that there could be more love and understanding among God's people. The fact that we are going to be together in heaven ought to encourage us to love each other on earth. This is one reason why Christ has already given us His glory within. "And the glory which Thou gavest Me I have given them; that they may be one, even as We are one" (John 17:22). As the poet put it:

> To live above, with saints we love,
>> Will certainly be glory.
> To live below, with saints we know,
>> Well, that's another story!

The hope of seeing Christ and going to heaven is not only a motivation for faith and love, but it is also a motivation for holy living. "And every man that hath this hope in Him purifieth himself, even as He is pure" (1 John 3:3). When I was a young Christian, an older friend warned me, "Don't be caught doing anything that would embarrass you if Jesus returned!" That is a rather negative view of the promise of heaven, even though it does have some merit. In fact, John warns us that if we do not abide in Christ (keep in fellowship with Him in obedience), we may be ashamed when He returns (1 John 2:28).

But there is a positive side to this truth. We should keep our lives clean so that when Jesus Christ *does* return, nothing will cloud our first meeting with Him. We will enter into the joy and glory of His presence with confidence and love! Peter called this a "rich welcome" into the everlasting kingdom (2 Peter 1:11, NIV).

The hope of heaven is also an encouragement in

times of suffering (1 Peter 1:4-9). As believers, we have our share of suffering; but in the midst of trials, we can rejoice "with joy unspeakable and full of glory" (1 Peter 1:8). When unbelievers suffer, they get discouraged and they want to give up. But when Christians suffer, their faith can become stronger and their love can deepen because their hope shines brighter.

How do we know that we have this hope? The promise is given in "the word of the truth of the Gospel" (Col. 1:5). We believers do not have to "work up" a good feeling of hope. God's unchanging Word assures us that our hope is secure in Christ. In fact, this hope is compared to an anchor (Heb. 6:19) that can never break or drift.

No wonder Paul was thankful for the believers in Colossae! God had given Paul "special miracles" at Ephesus (Acts 19:11). But no miracle is greater than the salvation of the lost sinner. Through the faithful witness of Epaphras, God performed miracles of grace in Colossae.

Have you experienced the miracle of salvation?

If you have, then keep growing and being fruitful for the Lord. The same Word that gave you life when you trusted Christ will continue to nourish that life and make you a faithful, fruitful Christian.

Are there any "Gospel miracles" of grace taking place where you live?

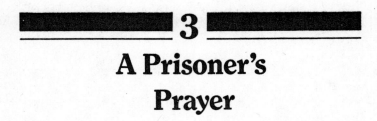

3

A Prisoner's Prayer

Colossians 1:9-12

The prayers in Paul's prison letters are certainly unique. To begin with, he prays for others and not for himself. The requests in his prayers center on *spiritual* blessings, not on material or physical matters. Of course, it is not wrong to pray about physical or material needs. But spiritual needs are vastly more important.

How would you pray for a group of people you had never seen? All that Paul knew about the believers in Colossae he learned from their faithful pastor, Epaphras. Paul knew of the false teaching that was threatening the church, so he centered his praying on that problem. In his prayer, Paul made three requests.

He Prayed for Spiritual Intelligence (Col. 1:9)

The false teachers promised the Colossian believers that they would be "in the know" if they accepted the new doctrines. Words like *knowledge, wisdom,* and *spiritual understanding* were a part of their religious vocabulary; so Paul used these words in his prayer.

Satan is so deceptive! He likes to borrow Christian vocabulary, but he does not use the Christian dictionary! Long before the false teachers had adopted these terms, the words had been in the Christian vocabulary.

The phrase, *for this cause,* relates the prayer to what Paul had written in verse 6: ". . . and knew the grace of God in truth." The report from Epaphras convinced Paul that these believers truly knew Christ and were born again. But there was much more to learn *from* Him and *about* Him! "You do not need a new spiritual experience," Paul was saying. "You only need to grow in the experience you have already had."

When a person is born into God's family by faith in Jesus Christ, he is born with all that he needs for growth and maturity. This is the theme of Colossians: "And you are complete in Him" (2:10). No other experience is needed than the new birth. "Do not look for something new," Paul warned the church. "Continue to grow in that which you received at the beginning" (author's paraphrase).

Every believer needs to have "the knowledge of His will." The Greek word translated *knowledge* in this verse carries the meaning of "full knowledge." There is always more to learn about God and His will for our lives. No Christian would ever dare to say that he had "arrived" and needed to learn nothing more. Like the college freshman who handed in a 10-page report on "The History of the Universe," that Christian would only declare his ignorance.

The will of God is an important part of a successful Christian life. God wants us to *know* His will (Acts 22:14) and *understand* it (Eph. 5:17). God is not a distant dictator who issues orders and never explains. Because we are His friends, we can know what He is doing and why He is doing it (John 15:13-15). As we study His Word and pray, we discover new and exciting truths about God's will for His people.

The word *filled* is a key word in Colossians. It was also a key word in the teachings of the false teachers who had invaded the Colossian church. Paul used it many times. (See Col. 1:19, 25; 2:2, 9-10; 4:12, 17 [*Complete* = "filled full"]). The word carries the idea of being fully equipped. It was used to describe a ship that was ready for a voyage. The believer has in Christ all that he needs for the voyage of life. "And you are complete in Him" (Col. 2:10). "And of His fullness have all we received" (John 1:16).

In the language of the New Testament, to be *filled* means to be "controlled by." When we are filled with anger, we are controlled by anger. To be "filled with the Spirit" (Eph. 5:18) means to be "controlled by the Spirit." Paul's prayer, then, is that these believers might be controlled by the full knowledge of God's will.

But how does this take place? How can believers grow in the full knowledge of God's will? Paul's closing words of verse 9 tell us: "by means of all wisdom and spiritual insight" (literal translation). *We understand the will of God through the Word of God.* The Holy Spirit teaches us as we submit to Him (John 14:26; 16:13). As we pray and sincerely seek God's truth, He gives us through the Spirit the wisdom and insight that we need (Eph. 1:17).

The *general* will of God for all His children is given clearly in the Bible. The *specific* will of God for any given situation must always agree with what He has already revealed in His Word. The better we know God's general will, the easier it will be to determine His specific guidance in daily life. Paul did not encourage the Colossians to seek visions or wait for voices. He prayed that they might get deeper into God's Word and thus have greater wisdom and insight concerning God's will. He wanted them to have "all wisdom"—not that they would know everything, but that they would have all the wisdom necessary for making decisions and living to please God.

Spiritual intelligence is the beginning of a successful, fruitful Christian life. God puts no premium on ignorance. I once heard a preacher say, "I didn't never go to school. I'm just a igerant Christian, and I'm glad I is!" A man does not have to go to school to gain spiritual intelligence; but neither should he magnify his "igerance."

Great men of God like Charles Spurgeon, G. Campbell Morgan, and H.A. Ironside never had the privilege of formal Bible training. But they were devoted students of the Word, learning its deeper truths through hours of study, meditation, and prayer. The first step toward fullness of life is spiritual intelligence—growing in the will of God by knowing the Word of God.

He Prayed for Practical Obedience (Col. 1:10)

The false teachers in Colossae attracted people through their offer of "spiritual knowledge," but they did not relate this knowledge to life. In the

Christian life, knowledge and obedience go together. There is no separation between *learning* and *living*. The wisdom about which Paul prayed was not simply a head knowledge of deep spiritual truths (see 1:28; 2:3; 3:16; 4:5). True spiritual wisdom must affect the daily life. Wisdom and practical intelligence must go together (see Ex. 31:3; Deut. 4:6; 1 Cor. 1:19).

In my pastoral ministry, I have met people who have become intoxicated with "studying the deeper truths of the Bible." Usually they have been given a book or introduced to some teacher's tapes. Before long, they get so smart they become dumb! The "deeper truths" they discover only detour them from practical Christian living. Instead of getting burning hearts of devotion to Christ (Luke 24:32), they get big heads and start creating problems in their homes and churches. All Bible truths are practical, not theoretical. If we are growing in knowledge, we should also be growing in grace (2 Peter 3:18).

Two words summarize the practicality of the Christian life: *walk* and *work*. The sequence is important: first, wisdom; then walk; then work. I cannot work for God unless I am walking with Him; but I cannot walk with Him if I am ignorant of His will. The believer who spends time daily in the Word and prayer (Acts 6:4) will know God's will and be able to walk with Him and work for Him.

After all, our purpose in life is not to please ourselves, but to please the Lord. We should walk *worthy of our calling* (Eph. 4:1) and *worthy of the Gospel* (Phil. 1:27), which means we will walk *worthy of God* (1 Thes. 2:12). In short, we should walk to please God (1 Thes. 4:1).

It is not we who work for God; it is God who works in us and through us to produce the fruit of His grace (Phil. 2:12-13). Christian service is the result of Christian devotion. The work that we do is the outflow of the life that we live. It is by abiding in Christ that we can produce fruit (John 15:1ff).

God must make the worker before He can do the work. God spent 13 years preparing Joseph for his ministry in Egypt, and 80 years preparing Moses to lead Israel. Jesus spent 3 years teaching His disciples how to bear fruit; and even the learned Apostle Paul needed a "post-graduate course" in Arabia before he could serve God with effectiveness. A newborn babe can cry and make its presence known, but it cannot work. A new Christian can witness for Christ and even win others—but he must be taught to walk and learn God's wisdom before he is placed in an office of responsible ministry.

God's wisdom reveals God's will. As we obey God's will in our walk, we can work for Him and bear fruit. We will not just occasionally serve God; we will be "fruitful in every good work" (Col. 1:10). But there is a blessed by-product of this experience: "increasing in the knowledge of God" (v. 10). As we walk with God and work for God, we get to know Him better and better.

Our Christian lives desperately need *balance*. Certainly we get to know God better as we pray in our private rooms and as we meditate on His Word. But we also get to know Him as we walk in our daily lives and work to win others and help His people.

Worship and service are not competitive. They always go together. When He was ministering on

earth, our Lord retired to pray—then He went out
to serve. We need to avoid the extremes of im-
practical mysticism and fleshly enthusiasm. As we
spend time with God, we get to understand Him
and His will for our lives; and as we go out to obey
Him, we learn more.

Practical obedience means pleasing God, serving
Him, and getting to know Him better. Any doctrine
that isolates the believer from the needs of the
world around him is not spiritual doctrine.
Evangelist D.L. Moody often said, "Every Bible
should be bound in shoe-leather." Paul would
agree.

Paul has prayed that we might have spiritual
intelligence, and that this intelligence might result
in practical obedience. But there is a third request
that completes these first two; and without it, the
Christian life could not be mature.

He Prayed for Moral Excellence (Col. 1:11-12)

Wisdom and conduct should always be related to
moral character. One of the great problems in our
evangelical world today is the emphasis on "spiritual knowledge" and "Christian service," without
connecting these important matters to personal
character.

For example, some teachers and preachers claim
to have God's wisdom—yet they lack love and kindness and the other basic qualities that make the
Christian life beautiful and distinctive. Even some
"soul-winning Christians" are so busy serving God
that they cannot take time to check facts—so they
publish lies about other Christians. For some
months, I read a certain religious publication. But

when I discovered that they had no "Letters to the Editor" column (except for praise), and that they never published a correction or apologized for an error, I stopped reading the magazine.

Knowledge, conduct, service, and character must always go together. We know God's will that we might obey it; and, in obeying it, we serve Him and grow in Christian character. While none of us is perfectly balanced in these four factors, we ought to strive for that balance.

It is God's energy that empowers us. Verse 11 reads, in effect: "with all power being empowered according to the might of His glory." Paul used two different Greek words for God's energy: *dunamis* (from which we get our word *dynamite*) means "inherent power"; and *kratos* means "manifested power," power that is put forth in action. The grace of our Christian lives is but a result of God's power at work in our lives. Spiritual growth and maturity can come only as we yield to God's power and permit Him to work in us.

We usually think of God's glorious power being revealed in great feats of daring—the Israelites crossing the Red Sea, David leading a victorious army, or Paul raising the dead. But the emphasis here is on Christian character: patience, long-suffering, joyfulness, and thanksgiving. The inner victories of the soul are just as great, if not greater, than the public victories recorded in the annals of history. For David to control his temper when he was being maligned by Shimei was a greater victory than his slaying of Goliath (2 Sam. 16:5-13). "He who is slow to anger is better than the mighty, and he who rules his spirit, than he who captures a city" (Prov. 16:32, NASB).

The word *patience* means "endurance when

circumstances are difficult." It is the opposite of despondency. This word is never used in reference to God, for God does not face difficult circumstances. Nothing is impossible with God (Jer. 32:27).

Patience is an important characteristic of the maturing Christian life. If we do not learn to be patient, we are not likely to learn anything else. As believers, we are able to rejoice even in our tribulations, because we know that "tribulation brings about perseverance; and perseverance proven character; and proven character, hope" (Rom. 5:3-4, NASB).

We must never think that patience is complacency. Patience is *endurance in action*. It is not the Christian sitting in a rocking chair, waiting for God to do something. It is the soldier on the battlefield, keeping on when the going is tough. It is the runner on the race track, refusing to stop because he wants to win the race (Heb. 12:1).

Too many Christians have a tendency to quit when circumstances become difficult. The saintly Dr. V. Raymond Edman, late president of Wheaton College (Illinois), used to remind the students, "It is always too soon to quit."

I have often thought of that statement when I find myself in the midst of trying circumstances. It is not talent or training that guarantees victory: it is perseverance. "By perseverance the snail reached the ark," said Charles Spurgeon.

Along with patience, we need *long-suffering*. This word means "self-restraint" and is the opposite of revenge. Patience has to do primarily with circumstances, while long-suffering has to do with people. God is long-suffering toward people because of His love and grace (2 Peter 3:9). Long-suffering is one fruit of the Spirit (Gal. 5:22). It is among the "grace garments" that the believer should wear on his soul (Col. 3:12).

It is amazing how people can patiently endure trying circumstances, only to lose their tempers with a friend or loved one. Moses was patient during the contest with Pharaoh in Egypt. But he lost his temper with his own people and, as a result, forfeited his right to enter the Promised Land (Num. 20). "Like a city that is broken into and without walls is a man who has no control over his spirit" (Prov. 25:28, NASB).

Patience and long-suffering go together if we are growing spiritually. Paul listed them as the marks of the true minister of Jesus Christ (2 Cor. 6:4-6). Certainly, Paul displayed these graces in his own life (2 Tim. 3:10). The great example of patience and long-suffering in the Old Testament is Job (James 5:10-11). In the New Testament, of course, it is Jesus Christ.

It is simple for God to perform miracles in the realms of the material or physical, because everything in creation obeys His command. Jesus could heal Malchus' ear, but He could not automatically change Peter's heart and remove the hatred and violence that was in it (Luke 22:50-51). God could bring water out of the rock, but He could not force Moses to be patient.

A pastor often visited a Christian young man who had been badly burned. The young man had to lie still for hours, and it was difficult for him to perform even the basic functions of life.

"I wish God would do a miracle and heal me," the young man said to his pastor one day.

"God is doing a miracle," the pastor replied, "but not the kind you are looking for. I have watched you grow in patience and kindness during these weeks. That, to me, is a greater miracle than the healing of your body."

God's power is evidenced in our lives not only in our patience and long-suffering, but also in our *joyfulness*. When circumstances are difficult, we should exhibit *joyful* patience; and when people are hard to live with, we should reveal *joyful* long-suffering. There is a kind of patience that "endures but does not enjoy." Paul prayed that the Colossian Christians might experience *joyful* patience and long-suffering.

We often use the words *joy* and *happiness* interchangeably, but a distinction should be made. Happiness often depends on happenings. If circumstances are encouraging and people are kind, we are happy. But joy is independent of both circumstances and people. The most joyful epistle Paul wrote was Philippians, and he wrote it from jail as he faced the possibility of being martyred for his faith.

Only God's Spirit, working within us, can give us joy in the midst of problem circumstances and problem people. "The fruit of the Spirit is . . . joy" (Gal. 5:22). Joy is not something that we ourselves "work up"; it is something the Spirit Himself "works in"—"joy in the Holy Spirit" (Rom. 14:17, NIV).

I can recall times in my life when all the circumstances around me pointed to difficulty and possible defeat. Yet my heart was filled with a spiritual joy that could only come from God. Sad to say, I also remember times (far too many!) when I gave in to the problems around me, and I lost both the joy and the victory.

The fourth evidence of God's power in our lives is *thankfulness*. Christians who are filled with the

Holy Spirit will be joyful and thankful (Eph. 5:18-20). When we lose our joy, we start complaining and becoming critical.

The Colossian epistle is filled with thanksgiving. Paul gave thanks for the church in Colossae (Col. 1:3), and he prayed that they might grow in their own thanksgiving to God (1:12). The Christian life should abound with thanksgiving (2:7). One of the evidences of spiritual growth in our Bible study is thanksgiving (3:15-17). Our prayers should always include thanksgiving (4:2). The Christian who is filled with the Spirit, filled with the Word, and watching in prayer will prove it by his attitude of appreciation and thanksgiving to God.

Some people are appreciative by nature, but some are not; and it is these latter people who especially need God's power to express thanksgiving. We should remember that every good gift comes from God (James 1:17) and that He is (as the theologians put it) "the Source, Support, and End of all things." The very breath in our mouths is the free gift of God.

Just a short drive from my home is the campus of Northwestern University in Evanston, Illinois. Years ago, the school had a life-saving squad that assisted passengers on the Lake Michigan boats. On September 8, 1860, a passenger boat, the *Lady Elgin,* floundered near Evanston, and a ministerial student, Edward Spencer, personally rescued 17 persons. The exertion of that day permanently damaged his health and he was unable to train for the ministry. When he died some years later, it was noted that not 1 of the 17 persons he had saved ever came to thank him.

Thankfulness is the opposite of selfishness. The selfish person says, "I *deserve* what comes to me!

Other people *ought* to make me happy!" But the mature Christian realizes that life is a gift from God, and that the blessings of life come only from His bountiful hand.

Of course, the one blessing that ought to move us constantly to thanksgiving is that God has made us "meet [fit] to be partakers of the inheritance of the saints in light" (Col. 1:12). The word *fit* means "qualified": God has qualified us for heaven! And, while we are waiting for Christ to return, we enjoy our share of the spiritual inheritance that we have in Him (Eph. 1:11, 18-23).

In the Old Testament, God's people had an *earthly* inheritance, the land of Canaan. Christians today have a *spiritual* inheritance in Christ. Canaan is not a picture of heaven, for there will be no battles or defeats in heaven. Canaan is a picture of our *present* inheritance in Christ. We must claim our inheritance by faith as we step out on the promises of God (Josh. 1:1-9). Day by day, we claim our blessings; and this makes us even more thankful to the Lord.

As we review this marvelous prayer, we can see how penetrating it is. We need spiritual intelligence if we are going to live to please God. We also need practical obedience in our walk and work. But the result of all of this must be spiritual power in the inner man, power that leads to joyful patience and long-suffering, with thanksgiving.

Have you been praying this way lately?

4

Crown Him
Lord of All!

Colossians 1:13-20

The false teachers in Colossae, like the false teachers of our own day, would not *deny* the importance of Jesus Christ. They would simply *dethrone* Him, giving Him prominence but not preeminence. In their philosophy, Jesus Christ was but one of many "emanations" that proceeded from God and through which men could reach God. It was this claim that Paul refuted in this section.

Probably no paragraph in the New Testament contains more concentrated doctrine about Jesus Christ than this one. We can keep ourselves from going on a detour if we remember that Paul wrote to prove the preeminence of Christ, and he did so by using four unanswerable arguments.

Christ Is the Saviour (Col. 1:13-14)

Man's greatest problem is sin—a problem that can never be solved by a philosopher or a religious teacher. Sinners need a Saviour. These two verses present a vivid picture of the four saving actions of Christ on our behalf.

He delivered us (1:13a). This word means "rescued from danger." We could not deliver ourselves from the guilt and penalty of sin, but Jesus could and did deliver us. We were in danger of spending eternity apart from God. The sword of God's judgment was hanging over our heads!

But this deliverance involved something else: we were delivered from the authority of Satan and the powers of darkness. The Gnostic false teachers believed in an organization of evil spirits that controlled the world (see Col. 1:16; 2:10, 15): angels, archangels, principalities, powers, virtues, dominions, and thrones. John Milton used these titles when describing Satan's forces in his classic *Paradise Lost.*

He translated us (1:13b). This word was used to describe the deportation of a population from one country into another. History records the fact that Antiochus the Great transported at least 2,000 Jews from Babylonia to Colossae.

Jesus Christ did not release us from bondage, only to have us wander aimlessly. He moved us into His own kingdom of light and made us victors over Satan's kingdom of darkness. Earthly rulers transported the defeated people, but Jesus Christ transported the winners.

The phrase *His dear Son* can be translated "the Son of His love." At the baptism and transfiguration of Jesus Christ, the Father declared that Jesus was His "beloved Son" (Matt. 3:17; 17:5). This fact reminds us of the price the Father paid when He gave His Son for us. It also reminds us that His kingdom is a kingdom of love as well as a kingdom of light.

The experience of Israel in the Old Testament is an illustration of this spiritual experience; for God delivered them from the bondage of Egypt and took them into the Promised Land of their inheritance. God brings us out that He might bring us in.

He redeemed us (1:14a). This word means "to release a prisoner of the payment of a ransom." Paul did not suggest that Jesus paid a ransom to Satan in order to rescue us from the kingdom of darkness. By His death and resurrection, Jesus met the holy demands of God's Law. Satan seeks to accuse us and imprison us because he knows we are guilty of breaking God's Law. But the ransom has been paid on Calvary, and through faith in Jesus Christ, we have been set free.

He has forgiven us (1:14b). Redemption and forgiveness go together (Eph. 1:7). The word translated *forgiveness* means "to send away" or "to cancel a debt." Christ has not only set us free and transferred us to a new kingdom, but He has cancelled every debt so that we cannot be enslaved again. Satan cannot find anything in the files that will indict us!

In recent years, the church has rediscovered the freedom of forgiveness. God's forgiveness of sinners is an act of His grace. We did not deserve to be forgiven, nor can we earn forgiveness. Knowing that we are forgiven makes it possible for us to fellowship with God, enjoy His grace, and seek to do His will. Forgiveness is not an excuse for sin; rather, it is an encouragement for obedience. And, because we have been forgiven, we can forgive others (Col. 3:13). The Parable of the Unforgiving Servant makes it clear that an unforgiving spirit always leads to bondage (Matt. 18:21-35).

Jesus Christ is preeminent in salvation. No other person could redeem us, forgive us, transfer us out of Satan's kingdom into God's kingdom, and do it wholly by grace. The phrase "through His blood" reminds us of the cost of our salvation. Moses and the Israelites only had to shed the blood of a lamb to be delivered from Egypt. But Jesus had to shed His blood to deliver us from sin.

Christ Is the Creator (Col. 1:15-17)

The false teachers were very confused about creation. They taught that matter was evil, including the human body. They also taught that Jesus Christ did not have a real body since this would have put Him in contact with evil matter. The results of these false teachings were tragic, including extreme asceticism on the one hand and unbridled sin on the other. After all, if your body is sinful, you either enjoy it or you try to enslave it.

In this section, Paul explained the fourfold relationship of Jesus Christ to creation.

He existed before creation (1:15). The term *firstborn* does not refer to time, but to place or status. Jesus Christ was not the first being created, since He Himself is the Creator of all things. *Firstborn* simply means "of first importance, of first rank." Solomon was certainly not born first of all of David's sons, yet he was named the firstborn (Ps. 89:27). *Firstborn of all creation* means "priority to all creation." Jesus Christ is not a created being; He is eternal God.

Paul used the word *image* to make this fact clear. It means "an exact representation and revelation." The writer to the Hebrews affirms that Jesus Christ is "the express image of His person" (Heb. 1:3). Jesus was able to say, "He that hath seen Me, hath seen the Father" (John 14:9). In His essence, God is invisible; but Jesus Christ has revealed Him to us (John 1:18). Nature reveals the existence, power, and wisdom of God; but nature cannot reveal the very essence of God to us. It is only in Jesus Christ that the invisible God is revealed perfectly. Since no mere creature can perfectly reveal God, Jesus Christ must be God.

He created all things (1:16). Since Christ created all things, He Himself is uncreated. The word *for* that introduces this verse could be translated "because." Jesus Christ is the Firstborn of all *because* He created all things. It is no wonder that the winds and waves obeyed Him, and diseases and death fled from Him, for He is Master over all. "All things were made by Him" (John 1:3). This includes all things in heaven and earth, visible and invisible. All things are under His command.

All things exist for Him (1:16b). Everything exists *in* Him, *for* Him, and *through* Him. Jesus Christ is the Sphere in which they exist, the Agent through which they came into being, and the One for whom they were made.

Paul's use of three different prepositions is one way of refuting the philosophy of the false teachers. For centuries, the Greek philosophers had taught that everything needed a primary cause, an instrumental cause, and a final cause. The primary cause is the plan, the instrumental cause the power, and the final cause the purpose. When it comes to creation, Jesus Christ is the primary cause (He planned it), the instrumental cause (He produced it), and the final cause (He did it for His own pleasure).

If everything in creation exists *for* Him, then nothing can be evil of itself (except for Satan and fallen angels; even those God uses to accomplish His will). Gnostic regulations about using God's creation are all foolish (Col. 2:20-23). It also means that God's creation, even though under bondage to sin (Rom. 8:22), can be used for God's glory and enjoyed by God's people (1 Tim. 6:17).

He holds all things together (1:17). "In Him all things hold together" (NIV). A guide took a group of people through an atomic laboratory and explained how all matter was composed of rapidly moving electric particles. The tourists studied models of molecules and were amazed to learn that matter is made up primarily of space. During the question period, one visitor asked, "If this is the way matter works, what holds it all together?" For that, the guide had no answer.

But the Christian has an answer: Jesus Christ! Because "He is before all things," He can hold all things together. Again, this is another affirmation that Jesus Christ is God. Only God exists before all of creation, and only God can make creation cohere. To make Jesus Christ less than God is to dethrone Him.

It used to bother me to sing the familiar song, "This Is My Father's World." I thought Satan and sin were in control of this world. I have since changed my mind, and now I sing the song with joy and victory. Jesus Christ made all things, He controls all things, and by Him all things hold together. Indeed, this *is* my Father's world!

Christ Is the Head of the Church (Col. 1:18)

There are many images of the church in the New Testament, and the body is one of the most important (Rom. 12:4ff; 1 Cor. 12:14; Eph. 4:8-16). No denomination or local assembly can claim to be "the body of Christ," for that body is composed of *all* true believers. When a person trusts Christ, he is immediately baptized by the Holy Spirit into this body (1 Cor. 12:12-13). The baptism of the Spirit is not a postconversion experience—for it occurs the instant a person believes in Jesus Christ.

Each Christian is a member of this spiritual body, and Jesus Christ is the Head. In Greek usage, the word *head* meant "source" and "origin" as well as "leader, ruler." Jesus Christ is the Source of the church, His body, and the Leader. Paul called Him "the Beginning," which tells us that Jesus Christ has priority in time as far as His church is concerned. The term *beginning* can be translated "originator."

No matter which name you select, it will affirm the preeminence of Jesus Christ in the church. The church had its origin in Him, and today it has its operation in Him. As the Head of the church, Jesus Christ supplies it with life through His Spirit. He gives gifts to men, and then places these gifted people in His church that they might serve Him where they are needed. Through His Word, Jesus Christ nourishes and cleanses the church (Eph. 5:25-30).

No believer on earth is the Head of the church. This position is reserved exclusively for Jesus Christ. Various religious leaders may have founded churches, or denominations; but only Jesus Christ is the Founder of the church which is His body. This church is composed of all true believers, and it was born at Pentecost. It was then that the Holy Spirit came and baptized the believers into one spiritual body.

The fact that there is "one body" in this world (Eph. 4:4) does not eliminate or minimize the need for *local* bodies of believers. The fact that I belong to the universal church does not release me from my responsibilities to the local church. I cannot minister to the whole church, but I can strengthen and build the church by ministering to God's people in a local assembly.

Jesus Christ is the Head of the church, and the Beginning of the church; and He is also the First-born from the dead. We saw this word *firstborn* in Colossians 1:15. Paul did not say that Jesus was the first person to be raised from the dead, for He was not. But He is the most important of all who have been raised from the dead; for without His resurrection, there could be no resurrection for others (1 Cor. 15:20ff).

It seems odd that Paul used the word *born* in connection with death, for the two concepts seem opposed to each other. But the tomb was a womb from which Christ came forth in victory, for the birthpangs of death could not hold Him (Acts 2:24). The Son was begotten in resurrection (Ps. 2:7; Acts 13:33).

This brings us to the theme of this entire section: "that in all things He might have the preeminence" (Col. 1:18). This was God's purpose in making His Son the Savior, Creator, and Head of the church. The word translated *preeminence* is used nowhere else in the New Testament. It is related to the word translated *firstborn,* and it magnifies the unique position of Jesus Christ. "Christ is all, and in all" (Col. 3:11).

In 1893, the World's Columbian Exposition was held in Chicago, and more than 21 million people visited the exhibits. Among the features was a "World Parliament of Religions," with represen-tatives of the world's religions, meeting to share their "best points" and perhaps come up with a new religion for the world.

Evangelist D.L. Moody saw this as a great opportunity for evangelism. He used churches, rented theaters, and even rented a circus tent (when the show was not on) to present the Gospel of Jesus Christ. His friends wanted Moody to attack the "Parliament of Religions," but he refused. "I am going to make Jesus Christ so attractive," he said, "that men will turn to Him." Moody knew that Jesus Christ was the preeminent Saviour, not just one of many "religious leaders" of history. The "Chicago Campaign" of 1893 was probably the greatest evangelistic endeavor in D.L. Moody's life, and thousands came to Christ.

But the false teachers of Colossae could never give Jesus Christ the place of preeminence; for, according to their philosophy, Jesus Christ was only one of many "emanations" from God. He was not the only Way to God (John 14:6); rather, He was but one rung on the ladder! It has well been said, "If Jesus Christ is not Lord of all, He cannot be Lord at all."

We have now studied three arguments for the preeminence of Jesus Christ: He is the Saviour, He is the Creator, and He is the Head of the church. These arguments reveal His relationship with lost sinners, with the universe, and with believers. But what about His relationship with God the Father?

He Is the Beloved of the Father (Col. 1:19-20)

Paul had already called Jesus Christ "His dear Son" (v. 13). Those who have trusted Jesus Christ as their Saviour are "accepted in the Beloved" (Eph. 1:6). For this reason, God can call *us* His beloved (Col. 3:12).

Then Paul took a giant step forward in his argument, for he declared that "all fullness" dwelt in Jesus Christ! The word translated "fullness" is the Greek word *pleroma* (pronounced "play-RO-ma"). It was a technical term in the vocabulary of the Gnostic false teachers. It meant "the sum total of all the divine power and attributes." We have already noted that Paul used this important word eight times in the Colossian letter, so he was meeting the false teachers on their own ground.

The word *dwell* is equally important. It means much more than merely "to reside." The form of the verb means "to be at home permanently." The late Dr. Kenneth S. Wuest, noted Greek expert, pointed out in his excellent commentary on Colossians that the verb indicates that this fullness was "not something added to His Being that was not natural to Him, but that it was part of His essential Being as part of His very constitution, and that permanently" (*Ephesians and Colossians in the Greek New Testament,* Eerdmans, p. 187).

The Father would not permanently give His *pleroma* to some created being. The fact that it "pleased the Father" to have His fullness in Christ is proof that Jesus Christ is God. "And of His [Christ's] fullness have all we received" (John 1:16). "For in Him [Jesus Christ] dwelleth all the fullness of the Godhead bodily" (Col. 2:9).

Because Jesus Christ is God, He is able to do what no mere man could ever do: reconcile lost sinners to a holy God. When the first man and woman sinned, they declared war on God; but God did not declare war on them. Instead, God sought

Adam and Eve; and He provided a covering for their sins.

The natural mind of the unsaved sinner is at war with God (Rom. 8:7). The sinner may be sincere, religious, and even moral; but he is still at war with God.

How can a holy God ever be reconciled with sinful man? Can God lower His standards, close His eyes to sin, and compromise with man? If He did, the universe would fall to pieces! God must be consistent with Himself and maintain His own holy Law.

Perhaps man could somehow please God. But by nature, man is separated from God; and by his deeds, he is alienated from God (Col. 1:21). The sinner is "dead in trespasses and sins" (Eph. 2:1ff), and therefore is unable to do anything to save himself or to please God (Rom. 8:8).

If there is to be reconciliation between man and God, the initiative and action must come from God. It is *in Christ* that God was reconciled to man (2 Cor. 5:19). But it was not the incarnation of Christ that accomplished this reconciliation, nor was it His example as He lived among men. It was through His *death* that peace was made between God and man. He "made peace through the blood of His cross" (Col. 1:20).

Of course, the false teachers offered a kind of reconciliation between man and God. However, the reconciliation they offered was not complete or final. The angels and the "emanations" could in some way bring men closer to God, according to the Gnostic teachers. But the reconciliation we have in Jesus Christ is perfect, complete, and final. More than that, the reconciliation in Christ *involves the whole universe!* He reconciles "all things unto because of their disobedience to God's holy Law. In Bible days, financial records were often kept on parchment, and the writing could be washed off. This is the picture Paul painted.

How could a holy God be just in cancelling a debt? In this way His Son paid the full debt when He died on the cross. If a judge sets a man free who is guilty of a crime, the judge cheapens the law and leaves the injured party without restitution. God paid sin's debt when He gave His Son on the cross, and He upheld the holiness of His own Law.

But Jesus Christ did even more than cancel the debt: He took the Law that condemned us and set it aside so that we are no longer under its dominion. We are "delivered from the Law" (Rom. 7:6). We "are not under the Law, but under grace" (Rom. 6:14). This does not mean that we are lawless, because the righteousness of the Law is fulfilled in us as we walk in the power of the Spirit (Rom. 8:4). Our relationship with Jesus Christ enables us to obey God out of love, not out of slavish fear.

Victorious in Him (2:15). Jesus not only dealt with sin and the Law on the cross, but He also dealt with Satan. Speaking about His crucifixion, Jesus said, "Now is the judgment of this world; now shall the prince of this world be cast out" (John 12:31). The death of Christ on the cross looked like a great victory for Satan, but it turned out to be a great defeat from which Satan cannot recover.

Jesus had three great victories on the cross. First, He "disarmed the powers and authorities" (Col. 2:15, NIV), stripping Satan and his army of whatever weapons they held. Satan cannot harm the believer who will not harm himself. It is when we cease to watch and pray (as did Peter) that Satan can use his weapons against us.

Himself . . . things in earth, or things in heaven"
(v. 20).

However, we must not conclude wrongly that
universal reconciliation is the same as universal
salvation. "Universalism" is the teaching that all
beings, including those who have rejected Jesus
Christ, will one day be saved. This was not what
Paul believed. "Universal restorationism" was not
a part of Paul's theology, for he definitely taught
that sinners needed to believe in Jesus Christ to be
saved (2 Thes. 1).

Paul wrote that Christ has solved the sin problem
on the cross once and for all. This means that one
day God can bring together in Christ all that belong to Him (Eph. 1:9-10). He will be able to
glorify believers and punish unbelievers, *and do it
justly*, because of Christ's death on the cross. No
one—not even Satan—can accuse God of doing
wrong, because sin has been effectively dealt with
on the cross.

If Jesus Christ is only a man, or only an emana-
tion from God, He cannot reconcile God and man.
The only arbitrator who can bring God and man
together is One who is *both God and Man himself*.
Contrary to what the Gnostics taught, Jesus Christ
was a true human being with a real body. He was
God in human flesh (John 1:14). When He died
on the cross, He met the just demands of the Law
because He paid the penalty for man's sins (1 Peter
2:24). Reconciliation has been completed on the
Cross (Rom. 5:11).

A man once came to see me because he had
difficulties at home. He was not a very well-
educated man and sometimes got his words confused. He told me that he and his wife were having
"martial problems" when he meant to say "marital

problems." (Later I found out that they really were "at war" with each other, so maybe he was right after all!) But the word that caught my attention was in this sentence: "Pastor, me and my wife need a re-cancellation."

He meant to say *reconciliation,* but the word *re-cancellation* was not a bad choice. There can be peace and a reunion of those who are at war *only when sin has been cancelled.* As sinners before a righteous God, we need a "re-cancellation." Our sins were cancelled on the cross.

As we review this profound section (and this study has only scratched the surface), we notice several important truths.

First, Jesus Christ has taken care of *all things.* All things were created by Him and for Him. He existed before all things, and today He holds all things together. He has reconciled all things through the Cross. No wonder Paul declared that "in all things He might have the preeminence" (Col. 1:18).

Second, all that we need is Jesus Christ. We have all of God's fullness in Him, and we are "filled full" (complete) in Him (2:10). There is no need to add anything to the Person or work of Jesus Christ. To add anything is to take away from His glory. To give Him prominence instead of pre-eminence is to dethrone Him.

Third, God is pleased when His Son, Jesus Christ, is honored and given preeminence. There are people who tell us they are Christians, but they ignore or deny Jesus Christ. "We worship the Father," they tell us, "and that is all that is necessary."

But Jesus made it clear that *the Son* is to be worshiped as well as the Father. ". . . that all may honor the Son just as they honor the Father. He who does not honor the Son does not honor the Father, who sent Him" (John 5:23-24, NIV).

The late Dr. M.R. DeHaan, noted radio Bible teacher, told about a preacher who was confronted by a cultist who rejected the deity of Jesus Christ.

"Jesus cannot be the eternal Son of God, for a father is always older than his son," the man argued. "If the Father is not eternal, then He is not God. If Jesus is His Son, then He is not eternal."

The preacher was ready with an answer. "The thing that makes a person a father is having a son. But if God is the *eternal* Father, then He must have an *eternal* Son! This means that Jesus Christ is eternal—and that He is God!"

Jesus Christ is the Saviour, the Creator, the Head of the church, and the Beloved of the Father. He is eternal God . . . and in our lives He deserves to have the preeminence.

Is Jesus Christ preeminent in your life?

5

One Man's
Ministry

Colossians 1:21—2:3

If you received a letter from a man you had never
met, a man who was a prisoner, accused of being a
troublemaker, how would you respond?

The Colossian believers faced that exact problem.
They knew that Paul had been instrumental in leading their pastor, Epaphras, to saving faith in Christ.
They also knew that Epaphras had gone to Rome to
consult with Paul and had not yet returned. The
church members had received Paul's letter, brought
to them by Tychicus and Onesimus. But the false
teachers in Colossae had been discrediting Paul
and causing doubts in the people's minds. "Why
listen to a man who is a political prisoner?" they
asked. "Can you trust him?"

Paul no doubt realized that this would be the
situation, so he paused in the first part of this letter
to give some words of explanation. He had been so
wrapped up in exalting Jesus Christ that he had not
shown any interest in writing about himself! In this
section, Paul explained his three ministries.

Sharing the Gospel (Col. 1:21-23)

Even though Paul had not personally evangelized Colossae, it was his ministry in Ephesus that led to the founding of the Colossian church. Paul was "made a minister" (1:25). A large part of his ministry consisted in preaching the good news of salvation through faith in Jesus Christ. His was a ministry of reconciliation (2 Cor. 5:17-21). Paul reviewed for his readers their own spiritual experience.

Their past alienation (1:21a). The word translated *alienated* means "estranged." These Gentiles in Colossae were estranged from God and separated from the spiritual blessings of Israel (Eph. 2:11ff). The gods that they worshiped were false gods, and their religious rituals could not take care of their sin or guilt.

But this estrangement was not only a matter of Gentile position; it was also a matter of sinful practices and attitudes. The Gentiles were *enemies*, which means they were "actively hostile to God." Even though they had not received a divine law, such as God gave to Israel, these Gentiles knew the truth about God through creation and conscience (Rom. 1:18ff). They could not plead ignorance before the bar of God's justice.

The enmity of their minds led to wicked works. Both in attitude and action, they were at war with God. "Because the carnal mind [the mind of the unbeliever] is enmity against God" (Rom. 8:7). This explains why the unbeliever must repent—change his mind—before he can be saved.

Their present reconciliation (1:21b-22). They did not reconcile themselves to God; it was God who took the initiative in His love and grace. The Father sent the Son to die on a cross that sinners might be reconciled to God. Jesus died for us when we were "without strength" (Rom. 5:6) and could do nothing for ourselves. He died for us "while we were yet sinners" and "when we were enemies" (Rom. 5:8, 10).

Paul emphasized the physical body of Jesus Christ that was nailed to the cross. The false teachers denied the Incarnation and taught that Jesus Christ did not have a real human body. Their philosophy that all matter was evil made it necessary for them to draw this false conclusion. But the New Testament makes it clear that Jesus *did* have a fully human body, and that He bore our sins on that body on the cross (1 Peter 2:24).

The purpose of this reconciliation is *personal holiness.* God does not make peace (Col. 1:20) so that we can continue to be rebels! He has reconciled us to Himself so that we may share His life and His holiness. We are presented to God "holy and unblameable and unreproveable" (v. 22).

The word *holy* is closely related to the word *saint.* Both of these words express the idea of "being set apart, being devoted to God." In the New Testament, saints are not dead people who during their lives performed miracles and never sinned. New Testament saints were living people who had trusted Jesus Christ. Paul wrote this letter to living saints (Col. 1:2).

Unblameable means "without blemish." The word was applied to the temple sacrifices which had to be without blemish. It is amazing that God looks at His children and sees no blemish on them! God chose us to be "holy and without blame" (Eph. 1:4).

Unreproveable means "free from accusation." Once we have been reconciled to God, no charges can be brought against us (Rom. 8:31-34). Satan, the accuser of the brethren (Rev. 12:1-12), would like to hurl charges at us; but God will not accept them (see Zech. 3). People may have accusations to bring against us, but they cannot change our relationship with God.

The most important thing in our Christian lives is not how we look in our own sight, or in the sight of others (1 Cor. 4:1-4)—but how we look in God's sight. I recall counseling a Christian who was in the habit of reminding herself of her past sins and failures. She seemed to enjoy having other people criticize her. I kept reminding her of what she was *in God's sight.* Her constant emphasis on her failures denied the work that Jesus Christ had done for her on the Cross. It took time, but eventually she accepted her wonderful new position in Christ and began to get victory over criticism and depression.

Paul's emphasis on our holy standing before God was certainly an attack on the false teachers, for they promised their followers a kind of "perfection" that nothing else could give. "You already have a perfect standing in Christ," Paul wrote, "so why seek for it anywhere else?"

Their future glorification (1:23). "The hope of the Gospel" means that blessed hope of our Lord's return (Titus 2:13). Paul had already mentioned this hope: "the hope which is laid up for you in heaven" (Col. 1:5). Later in the chapter, he called it "the hope of glory" (1:27).

There was a time when these Gentile Colossians were without hope (Eph. 2:12). The reason? They were without God. But when they were reconciled to God, they were given a wonderful hope of glory. All of God's children will one day be with

Christ in heaven (John 17:24). In fact, so secure is our future that Paul stated that we have *already been glorified!* (Rom. 8:30). All we are waiting for is the revelation of this glory when Jesus Christ returns (Rom. 8:17-19).

Paul's statement to the Colossians seems to cast a shadow on the assurance of our future glory (see Col. 1:23). Is it possible for a believer to lose his salvation? No, the *if* clause does not suggest doubt or lay down a condition by which we "keep up our salvation."

Paul used an architectural image in this verse— a house, firmly set on the foundation. The town of Colossae was located in a region known for earthquakes, and the word translated *moved away* can mean "earthquake stricken." Paul was saying, "If you are truly saved, and built on the solid foundation, Jesus Christ, then you will continue in the faith and nothing will move you. You have heard the Gospel and trusted Jesus Christ, and He has saved you."

In other words, we are not saved by continuing in the faith. But we continue in the faith and thus prove that we are saved. It behooves each professing Christian to test his own faith and examine his own heart to be sure he is a child of God (2 Cor. 13:5; 2 Peter 1:10ff).

Suffering for the Gentiles (Col. 1:24-27)

Paul's enemies made much of the fact that the great apostle was a prisoner of Rome. The false teachers in Colossae probably ridiculed Paul and used this as a weapon to fight the truth of the Gospel. But Paul turned this weapon around and used it to defeat his enemies and to build a closer relationship with the church in Colossae.

His rejoicing (1:24). "Instead of being ashamed of my suffering, I am rejoicing in it!" How could anyone rejoice in suffering? To begin with, Paul was suffering because of Jesus Christ. It was "the fellowship of His sufferings" (Phil. 3:10). Like the early apostles, Paul rejoiced that he was "counted worthy to suffer shame for His name" (Acts 5:41). A Christian should never suffer "as a thief or as an evil doer"; but it is an honor to "suffer as a Christian" (1 Peter 4:15-16). There is a special blessing and reward reserved for the faithful believer who suffers for the sake of Christ (Matt. 5:10-12).

Paul had a second cause for rejoicing in his suffering: he was suffering because of the Gentiles. Paul was the chosen apostle to the Gentiles (Eph. 3:1-13). In fact, he was a prisoner in Rome because of his love for the Gentiles. He was arrested in Jerusalem on false charges, and the Jews listened to his defense until he used the word *Gentiles* (see Acts 22:21ff). It was that word that infuriated them and drove them to ask for his execution. (The full account is given in Acts 21—28, and an exciting account it is.)

So the Gentile believers in Colossae had every reason to love Paul and be thankful for his special ministry to them. But there was a third cause for Paul's rejoicing: he was suffering for the sake of Christ's body, the church. There was a time when Paul had persecuted the church and caused it to suffer. But now Paul devoted his life to the care of the church. Paul did not ask, as do some believers, "What will *I* get out of it?" Instead he asked, "How much will God let me put into it?" The fact that

Paul was a prisoner did not stop him from ministering to the church.

It is important to note, however, that these sufferings had nothing to do with the sacrificial sufferings of Christ on the cross. Only the sinless Lamb of God could die for the sins of the world (John 1:29). Paul was "filling up in his turn the leftover parts of Christ's sufferings" (Col. 1:24, literal translation). The word *afflictions* refers to the "pressures" of life, the persecutions Paul endured. This word is never used in the New Testament for the sacrificial sufferings of Jesus Christ.

The sacrificial sufferings of Christ are over, but His body, the church, experiences suffering because of its stand for the faith. The Head of the church in heaven feels the sufferings that His people endure. ("Saul, Saul, why persecutest thou Me?" Acts 9:4) Paul was taking his turn in sharing these afflictions, and others would follow in his train. But Paul did not complain. "For as the sufferings of Christ abound in us, so our consolation also abounds by Christ" (2 Cor. 1:5).

Paul's responsibility (1:25-27). Had Paul compromised with the Jews and stopped ministering to the Gentiles, he could have been spared a great deal of suffering. But he could not abandon his calling just for personal safety and comfort. He had been made a minister by God; he had been given a "stewardship" (dispensation) and he had to be faithful to his calling (1 Cor. 4:2). It was not a matter of choice: he was called to fulfill the word of God. This can mean, "I must preach the Word fully and not compromise any truth." It can also mean, "I am commissioned by God's Word and I must be faithful to discharge my office."

Paul's special message regarding the Gentiles had

to do with what he called *the mystery*. To us today, a mystery is something eerie and perhaps frightening; but this was not the way the word was defined in Paul's day. The false teachers used this word to describe the inner secrets of their religions. A *mystery* is a "sacred secret," hidden in the past and now revealed by the Holy Spirit (see Eph. 3:1-13).

God called the nation of Israel to be His own people. He gave them His Law (including the priesthood and sacrifices), and He gave them a wonderful land. He promised them a King who would one day establish a glorious kingdom and fulfill the many promises made to Abraham and David. The Old Testament prophets wrote about a Messiah who would suffer, and a Messiah who would reign; and they could not explain the seeming contradiction (see 1 Peter 1:9-12). They did not understand that the Messiah first had to suffer before He could enter into glory (Luke 24:13-27).

Jesus Christ came to earth, was rejected by His people, and was crucified. He arose again and returned to heaven. Did this mean that God's promised kingdom for Israel was now abandoned? No, because God had initiated a new program— His *mystery*—that was not explained by the Old Testament prophets. The mystery is that today God is uniting Jews and Gentiles in the church (Eph. 2:11-22). When the church is completed, then Jesus Christ will return and take His people to heaven (1 Thes. 4:13-18). Then He will again deal with Israel as a nation and establish the promised kingdom (Acts 15:12-18).

Imagine what this message meant to the Gentiles. They were no longer excluded from the glory and riches of God's grace! During the Old Testament dispensation, a Gentile had to become a Jewish proselyte in order to share in the blessings of Israel. But in the new dispensation, Jews and Gentiles alike are saved by faith in Jesus Christ (Rom. 10:12-13). No wonder the Jewish false teachers opposed Paul: he dared to say, "There is no difference!"

We who have grown up in somewhat Christian surroundings have a tendency to take all of this for granted. But think of the excitement this message must have generated in a church composed of new believers who had no background in the church. Once they were outside the covenants of God, but now they were members of His family. Once they were living in spiritual ignorance and death, but now they were alive and sharing in the riches of God's wisdom in Christ. Once they had no hope, but now they had a glorious hope because Christ now lived within! It would be good for us today to recapture some of that "first love" excitement.

I was privileged to minister in Africa for three weeks, and there I was introduced to some of the finest Christians I have ever met. I taught the Word to over 500 national pastors in Kenya for almost a week, and each service was a challenge and blessing to me. Many of the pastors still had the marks of paganism and idolatry on their bodies; yet their faces were aglow with the joy of the Lord. I went to Africa to minister to them, *but they ministered to me!* They reminded me not to take for granted the glorious riches I have in Jesus Christ.

Striving for the Saints
(Col. 1:28—2:3)

We have met Paul the preacher, sharing the Gospel and Paul the prisoner, suffering for the Gentiles.

Now we meet Paul the prayer-warrior, striving in prayer for the individual saints that they might mature in the faith. The words *striving* (1:29) and *conflict* (2:1) are athletic terms. They refer to the strenuous effort put forth by the runner to win the race. Our English word *agony* comes from this Greek word.

Paul's instruction (1:28). *Whom* refers, of course, to Jesus Christ. "For we preach not ourselves, but Christ Jesus the Lord" (2 Cor. 4:5). The false teachers exalted themselves and their great "spiritual" attainments. They preached a system of teaching, but Paul preached a Person. The Gnostics preached philosophy and the empty traditions of men (Col. 2:8), but Paul proclaimed Jesus Christ. The false teachers had lists of rules and regulations (Col. 2:16, 20-21), but Paul presented Christ. What a difference in ministries!

Paul not only *preached* (the word means "to announce with authority as a herald"), but he also *warned*. While it is good to proclaim positive truth, it is also necessary to warn God's people against the lies of the enemy (Acts 20:31). In fact, God's people should be alert to warn one another (*admonish* in Col. 3:16, NIV). Paul considered himself a spiritual father to the local churches, and it was his duty to warn his children (1 Cor. 4:14).

But Paul was also a teacher of the truth. It is not enough to warn people; we must also teach them the positive truths of the Word of God. How far would we get in our travels if the highway signs told us where the roads were *not* going? Not very far! It is good to *win* a man to Christ, and then to *warn* him about the dangers ahead; but it is also important to *teach* that convert the basic truths of the Christian life.

Paul not only preached Christ, but he also "taught Christ," for in Christ are "all the treasures of wisdom and knowledge" (Col. 2:3). It was not necessary to introduce any new teaching, for all that a believer needs to know is related to Jesus Christ. "'Teaching every man in all wisdom'" was Paul's concern (Col. 1:28). Wisdom is the right use of knowledge. The false teachers promised to give people a "hidden wisdom" that would make them "spiritually elite." But all true spiritual wisdom is found only in Jesus Christ.

Paul's intent (1:28b). He wanted to present every believer "perfect in Christ Jesus." The word *perfect* was a favorite word with the Gnostic teachers. It described the disciple who was no longer a novice, but who had matured and was fully instructed in the secrets of the religion. Paul used it to mean "complete, mature in Christ." This is the goal of all preaching, warning, and teaching.

What are the evidences of this spiritual maturity? Paul described them next (Col. 2:2).

Encouragement—"that their hearts might be comforted." Our English word *encourage* means "with heart." To encourage people is to give them new heart. Shallow sympathy usually makes people feel worse, but true spiritual encouragement makes them feel better. It brings out the best in people.

Endearment—"being knit together in love." The mature Christian loves the brethren and seeks to be a peacemaker, not a troublemaker. He is a part of spiritual unity in the church. An immature person is selfish and causes division.

Enrichment—"unto all riches of the full assurance of understanding." Paul mentioned the riches of Christ earlier (Col. 1:27). Too many Christians are living like paupers when they could be living like

kings. Mature Christians do not complain about
what they don't have. Rather, they make use of the
vast resources that they *do* have in Jesus Christ.

Enlightenment—"full assurance of understanding." The mature believer has assurance in his heart
that he is a child of God. The spiritual knowledge
that he has in Christ constantly enlightens him
and directs him daily. I have often counseled believers who told me they lacked assurance of their
salvation. Invariably, they have been neglecting
God's Word and living in ignorance.

God wants us as His children to have "understanding" and "wisdom and knowledge" (2:2-3).
The word translated *understanding* literally means
"to place together." It is the ability to assess things.
Wisdom implies the ability to defend what we
understand. *Knowledge* suggests the ability to grasp
truth. All of these terms were also used by the
Gnostics.

Paul's intercession (1:29—2:1). "For this I labor
to the point of exhaustion, agonizing" is a literal
translation of the first part of Colossians 1:29.
What a picture of prayer! So much of our praying
is calm and comfortable, and yet Paul exerted his
spiritual muscles the way a Greek runner would
exert himself in the Olympic games. He also taught
Epaphras to pray the same way (Col. 4:12).

This does not mean that our prayers are more
effective if we exert all kinds of fleshly energy.
Nor does it mean that we must "wrestle with God"
and wear Him out before He will meet our needs.
Paul described a *spiritual* striving: it was *God's*
power at work in his life. True prayer is directed
to the Father (Matt. 6:9), through the Son (in His
name, John 14:13-14), in the power of the Holy
Spirit (Jude 20). When the Spirit is at work in

our lives, then we can pray mightily in the will of God.

How does the Spirit assist us in our praying? For one thing, the Spirit teaches us the Word and shows us the will of God (John 16:13-15). Prayer is not our trying to change God's mind. It is learning what is the mind of God and asking accordingly (1 John 5:14-15). The Holy Spirit constantly intercedes for us even though we do not hear His voice (Rom. 8:26-27). He knows the Father's will and He helps us pray in that will.

There are times when we simply do not feel like praying—and that is when we must pray the most! The Spirit gives us divine energy for prayer, in spite of the way we feel. The resurrection power of Jesus Christ is made available to us (Eph. 3:20-21).

In these verses Paul explained his ministry, and in so doing, he silenced the accusations of the enemy. He also stirred the affections of the believers as they realized how much Paul had done for them.

All of us are not called to be apostles, but each one of us does have a God-given ministry. We can share the Gospel and be soul-winners. We can suffer for Christ and fulfill the ministry God has given us. We can strive in prayer for God's people and encourage them to mature. Paul took time to minister to *individuals*; note the repetition of "every man" in Colossians 1:28. If we minister to only a few believers, we are helping the whole church.

Are you fulfilling your God-given ministry?

6

Saints Alive—
and Alert

Colossians 2:4-15

I recall a story about a pastor who was concerned about some unsavory businesses that had opened near a school. His protests finally led to a court case, and the defense attorney did all he could to embarrass the Gospel minister.

"Are you not a pastor?" the lawyer asked. "And doesn't the word *pastor* mean 'shepherd'?"

To this definition the minister agreed.

"Well, if you are a shepherd, why aren't you out taking care of the sheep?"

"Because today I'm fighting the wolves!" was the pastor's quick reply, and a good answer it was.

Knowing that there were enemies already attacking the church in Colossae, Paul offered encouragement. By heeding his admonitions, the Colossians would overcome their enemies.

Keep Making Spiritual Progress
(Col. 2:4-7)

In the Christian life, we never stand still: we either go forward or gradually slip backward. "Let us go on to maturity!" is the call we must obey (Heb. 6:1, literal translation). The Christian who is not making spiritual progress is an open target for the enemy to attack and destroy.

The need for progress (2:4). Satan is deceptive. He wants to lead believers astray, and to do this, he uses deceptive words. The Greek term used here describes the persuasive arguments of a lawyer. Satan is a liar (John 8:44) and by his lies he leads believers into the wrong path. It is important that we exercise spiritual discernment, and that we continue to grow in our knowledge of spiritual truth.

The nature of progress (2:5-7). In order to emphasize his admonition, Paul used several vivid pictures to illustrate spiritual progress.

The army (v. 5). The words *order* and *steadfastness* are military terms. They describe an army that is solidly united against the enemy. *Order* describes the arrangement of the army in ranks, with each soldier in his proper place. Not everybody can be a five-star general, but the general could never fight the battle alone. *Steadfastness* pictures the soldiers in battle formation, presenting a solid front to the enemy. Christians ought to make progress in discipline and obedience, just as soldiers on the battlefield.

The pilgrim (v. 6). The Christian life is compared to a pilgrimage, and believers must learn to walk. Paul had already encouraged his readers to "walk worthy of the Lord" (1:10), and later he used this image again (3:7; 4:5). In the Book of Ephesians, the companion letter to the Book of Colossians, Paul used the image at least seven times (Eph. 2:2, 10; 4:1, 17; 5:2, 8, 15).

We are to walk in Christ the same way we originally received Christ—*by faith*. The Gnostic teachers wanted to introduce some "new truths" for Christian maturity, but Paul denounced them. "You started with Christ and you must continue with Christ," Paul wrote. "You started with faith and you must continue with faith. This is the only way to make spiritual progress."

The tree (v. 7a). *Rooted* is an agricultural word. The tense of the Greek word means "once and for all having been rooted." Christians are not to be tumbleweeds that have no roots and are blown about by "every wind of doctrine" (Eph. 4:14). Nor are they to be "transplants" that are repeatedly moved from soil to soil. Once we are rooted by faith in Christ, there is no need to change the soil! The roots draw up the nourishment so that the tree can grow. The roots also give strength and stability.

The building (v. 7b). *Built up* is an architectural term. It is in the present tense: "being built up." When we trust Christ to save us, we are put on the foundation; from then on, we grow in grace. The word *edify* that is found often in Paul's letters simply means "to build up." To make spiritual progress means to keep adding to the temple to the glory of God.

The school (v. 7c). It is the Word of God that builds and strengthens the Christian. Epaphras had faithfully taught the Colossian believers the truth of the Word (1:7). But the false teachers were undermining that doctrine. Today, Christians who study the Word become established in the faith. Satan has a difficult time deceiving the Bible-taught believer.

The river (v. 7d). The word *abounding* is often used by Paul. It suggests the picture of a river overflowing its banks. Our first experience in the Lord is that of drinking the water of life by faith, and He puts within us an artesian well of living water (John 4:10-14). But that artesian well should become a "river of living water" (John 7:37-39) that grows deeper and deeper. The image of the river flowing from the sanctuary (Ezek. 47) getting deeper as it flows, probably is what Paul had in mind. Sad to say, many of us are making no progress—our lives are shallow trickles instead of mighty rivers.

Again, Paul mentioned "thanksgiving" (see Col. 1:3, 12). A thankful spirit is a mark of Christian maturity. When a believer is abounding in thanksgiving, he is really making progress!

By reviewing these pictures of spiritual progress, we see how the growing Christian can easily defeat the enemy and not be led astray. If his spiritual roots are deep in Christ, he will not want any other soil. If Christ is his sure foundation, he has no need to move. If he is studying and growing in the Word, he will not be easily enticed by false doctrine. And if his heart is overflowing with thanksgiving, he will not even consider turning from the fullness he has in Christ. A grounded, growing, grateful believer will not be led astray.

Watch Out for Spiritual Perils (Col. 2:8-10)

Paul continued the military image with this warning: "Beware lest any man carry you off as a captive" (literal translation). The false teachers did not go out and win the lost, no more than the cultists do today. They "kidnapped" converts from churches! Most of the people I have talked with who are members of anti-Christian cults were at one time associated with a Christian church of one denomination or another.

How is it possible for false teachers to capture people? The answer is simple: These "captives" are ignorant of the truths of the Word of God. They become fascinated by the philosophy and empty delusion of the false teachers. (This is not to say that *all* philosophy is wrong, because there is a Christian philosophy of life. The word simply means "to love wisdom.") When a person does not know the doctrines of the Christian faith, he can easily be captured by false religions.

This philosophy of the false teachers is "hollow and deceptive" (v. 8, NIV) for several reasons. To begin with, it is the tradition of men and not the truth of God's Word. The word *tradition* means that which is handed down"; and there is a true Christian tradition (2 Thes. 2:15; 3:6; 2 Tim. 2:2; 1 Cor. 15:3ff). The important thing about any teaching is its origin: did it come from God or from man? The religious leaders in our Lord's day had their traditions and were very zealous to obey them and protect them (Matt. 15:1-20). Even the Apostle Paul, before he met the Lord, was "exceedingly zealous of the traditions" (Gal. 1:14).

If a new Christian from a distant mission field were to visit many of our churches, he would probably be astounded at the ideas and practices we have that cannot be supported by God's Word. Our man-made traditions are usually more important to us than the God-given doctrines of the Scriptures! While it is not wrong to have church traditions that remind us of our godly heritage, we must be careful not to make these traditions equal to the Word of God.

The false teachers' traditions were "hollow and deceptive" for another reason: they involved "the rudiments of the world." The Greek word translated *rudiments* basically means "one of a row or series." It had several meanings attached to it: (1) the elementary sounds or letters, the A B Cs; (2) the basic elements of the universe, as in 2 Peter 3:10-12; (3) the basic elements of knowledge, the A B Cs of some system, as in Hebrews 5:12. But in ancient Greece, this word also meant "the elemental spirits of the universe, the angels that influenced the heavenly bodies." It was one of the words in the vocabulary of the religious astrology of that day.

The Gnostics believed that the angels and the heavenly bodies influenced people's lives. Paul's warnings to the Colossians about "new moon" and other religious practices determined by the calendar (Col. 2:16) may be related to this Gnostic teaching, although the Jewish people also watched the calendar (Gal. 4:10). One thing is certain: such teachings about demons and angels were not a part of true Christian doctrine. If anything, such teachings were satanic.

The fact that this teaching is not after Christ is sufficient to warn us against horoscopes, astral charts, Ouija boards, and other spiritist practices. The whole zodiac system is contrary to the teaching of the Word of God. The Christian who dabbles in mysticism and the occult is only asking for trouble.

Why follow empty philosophy when we have all fullness in Christ? This is like turning away from the satisfying river to drink at the dirty cisterns of the world (Jer. 2:13). Of course, the false teachers in Colossae did not ask the believers to forsake Christ. They asked them to make Christ a *part* of the new system. But this would only remove Him from His rightful place of preeminence.

So Paul gave the true and lasting antidote to all false teaching: "All fullness is in Christ, and you have been made full in Him. *Why, then, would you need anything else?*" (see Col. 2:9-10)

We have seen the word "fullness" (*pleroma*) before (1:19). It means "the sum total of all that God is, all of His being and attributes." This word was used by the Gnostics, but they did not give it the same meaning as did Paul. To them, the *pleroma* was the source of all the "emanations" through which men could come to God. The highest point in Gnostic religious experience was to share in the *pleroma*.

Of course, there are no emanations from God. The gulf between heaven and earth was bridged in the incarnation of Jesus Christ. He is declared to be "Emmanuel, God with us" (Matt. 1:23). Jesus Christ is the fullness of God, and that fullness dwells continually and permanently in Him *bodily*. Once again, Paul refuted the Gnostic doctrine that matter was evil and that Jesus did not have a human body.

When Jesus Christ ascended to heaven, He went in a human body. It was a glorified body, to be sure, but it was real. After His resurrection, our Lord was careful to assure His disciples that He was the same Person in the same body; He was not a ghost or a spirit. (See John 20:19-29.) There is a glorified Man in heaven! The God-Man, Jesus Christ, embodies the fullness of God!

Now, the remarkable thing is this: *every believer shares that fullness!* "And you are complete in Him" (Col. 2:10). The tense of the Greek verb indicates that this fullness is a permanent experience. Dr. Kenneth Wuest's very literal *Expanded Translation* reads, "And you are in Him, having been completely filled full with the present result that you are in a state of fullness."

When a person is born again into the family of God, he is born complete in Christ. His spiritual growth is not by *addition*, but by *nutrition*. He grows from the inside out. Nothing needs to be added to Christ because He already is the very fullness of God. As the believer draws on Christ's fullness, he is "filled unto all the fullness of God" (Eph. 3:19). What more does he need?

Indeed, there are spiritual perils that the Christian faces. The fundamental test of any religious teaching is, "Where does it put Jesus Christ —His Person and His work?" Does it rob Him of His fullness? Does it deny either His deity or His humanity? Does it affirm that the believer must have some "new experience" to supplement his experience with Christ? If so, that teaching is wrong and dangerous.

Draw upon Your Spiritual Provisions (Col. 2:11-15)

Remember that the false teaching that threatened the Colossian church was made up of several elements: Oriental mysticism, astrology, philosophy, and Jewish legalism. It is the latter element that Paul dealt with in this section of his letter. Apparently, the false teachers insisted that their converts submit to circumcision and obey the Old Testament law.

Gnostic legalism was not quite the same as the brand of legalism practiced by the Judaizers whom Paul refuted in his epistle to the Galatians. The Jewish teachers that Paul attacked in Galatians insisted that circumcision and obedience to the Law were necessary for salvation. (See Acts 15 for some background on this problem.) Gnostic legalism said that the Jewish law would help the believers become more spiritual. If they were circumcised, and if they watched their diets and observed the holy days, then they would become part of the "spiritual elite" in the church. Unfortunately, we have people with similar ideas in our churches today.

Paul made it clear that the Christian is not subject in any way to the Old Testament legal system, *nor can it do him any good spiritually.* Jesus Christ *alone* is sufficient for our every spiritual need, for all of God's fullness is in Him. We are identified with Jesus Christ because He is the Head of the body (Col. 1:18) and we are the members of the body (1 Cor. 12:12-13). Paul explained our fourfold identification with Jesus Christ that makes it not only unnecessary, but sinful for us to get involved in any kind of legalism.

Circumcised in Him (2:11). Circumcision was a sign of God's covenant with the Jewish people (Gen. 17:9-14). Though it was a physical operation, it had a spiritual significance. The trouble was, the Jewish people depended on the physical and not the spiritual. A mere physical operation could never convey spiritual grace (Rom. 2:25-29). Often in the Old Testament, God warned His people to turn from their sins and experience a *spiritual* circumcision of the heart (Deut. 10:16, 30:6; Jer. 4:4, 6:10; Ezek. 44:7). People make the same mistake today when they depend on some religious ritual to save them—such as baptism or the Lord's Supper.

It is not necessary for the believer to submit to circumcision, because he has already experienced a spiritual circumcision through his identification with Jesus Christ. But there is a contrast here between Jewish circumcision and the believer's spiritual circumcision in Christ:

Jews	Believers
External surgery	internal—the heart
part of the body	the whole "body of sins"
done by hands	done without hands
no spiritual help in conquering sin	enables them to overcome sin

When Jesus Christ died and rose again, He won a complete and final victory over sin. He not only died *for* our sins (salvation), but He "died *unto* sin" (sanctification; see Rom. 6:10ff). What the Law could not do, Jesus Christ accomplished for us. The old nature ("the body of the sins of the flesh") was put off—rendered inoperative—so that we need no longer be enslaved to its desires. The old sinful nature is not eradicated, for we can still sin (1 John 1:5—2:6). But the power has been broken as we yield to Christ and walk in the power of the Spirit.

Alive in Him (2:12-13). Here Paul used the illustration of baptism. Keep in mind that in the New Testament, the word *baptize* has both a literal and a figurative meaning. The literal meaning is "to dip, to immerse." The figurative meaning is "to be identified with." For example, the Jewish nation was "baptized unto Moses" when it went through the Red Sea (1 Cor. 10:1-2). There was no water involved in this baptism, because they went over on dry land. In this experience, the nation was identified with Moses.

Paul used the word *baptism* in a figurative sense in this section of his letter—for no amount of material water could bury a person with Christ or make him alive in Christ. Water baptism by immersion is a picture of this spiritual experience.

When a person is saved, he is immediately baptized by the Spirit into the body of Christ (1 Cor. 12:12-13) and identified with the Head, Jesus Christ. This identification means that *whatever happened to Christ also happened to us*. When He died, we died with Him. When He was buried, we were buried. When He arose again, we arose with Him—and we left the grave clothes of the old life behind (Col. 3:1-14).

All of this took place "through the faith of the operation of God" (v. 12). It was the power of God that changed us, not the power of water. The Spirit of God identified us with Jesus Christ, and we were buried with Him, raised with Him, and made alive with Him! (The Greek verbs are very expressive: co-buried, co-raised, and co-made alive.) Because God raised His Son from the dead, we have eternal life.

The practical application is clear: since we are identified with Christ, and He is the fullness of God, *what more do we need?* We have experienced the energy of God through faith in Christ, so why turn to the deadness of the Law? God has forgiven us all our trespasses (v. 13b) so that we have a perfect standing before Him.

Free from the Law in Him (2:14). Jesus not only took our sins to the cross (1 Peter 2:24), but He also took the Law to the cross and nailed it there, forever out of the way. The Law was certainly against us, because it was impossible for us to meet its holy demands. Even though God never gave the Ten Commandments to the Gentiles, the righteous demands of the Law—God's holy standards—were "written in their hearts" (Rom. 2:12-16).

When He shed His blood for sinners, Jesus Christ cancelled the huge debt that was against sinners

Second, Jesus "made a public spectacle" (v. 15, NIV) of the enemy, exposing Satan's deceit and vileness. In His death, resurrection, and ascension, Christ vindicated God and vanquished the devil.

His third victory is found in the word *triumph*. Whenever a Roman general won a great victory on foreign soil, took many captives and much loot, and gained new territory for Rome, he was honored by an official parade known as "the Roman triumph." Paul alluded to this practice in his second letter to the Corinthians (see 2 Cor. 2:14). Jesus Christ won a complete victory, and He returned to glory in a great triumphal procession (Eph. 4:8ff). In this, He disgraced and defeated Satan.

You and I share in His victory over the devil. We need not worry about the elemental forces that govern the planets and try to influence men's lives. The satanic armies of principalities and powers are defeated and disgraced! As we claim the victory of Christ, use the equipment He has provided for us (Eph. 6:10ff), and trust Him, we are free from the influence of the devil.

What a wonderful position and provision we have in Christ! Are we living up to it by faith?

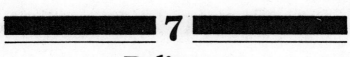

Believer, Beware!

Colossians 2:16-23

From the flashing red signals at a railroad crossing to the skull and crossbones on a bottle of rubbing alcohol, warnings are a part of daily life. Children must be taught to heed warnings, and adults must be reminded not to get too accustomed to them. Warnings are a matter of life or death.

The spiritual life also has its dangers and its warnings. Moses warned the Israelites to beware of forgetting the Lord once they got settled in the Promised Land (Deut. 6:12). The Lord Jesus often used the word *beware* (Matt. 7:15; Mark 12:38; Luke 12:15).

Paul had already warned about the false teachers (Col. 2:8). In this section of his letter, Paul gave three warnings for us to heed if we are to enjoy our fullness in Jesus Christ.

"Let No One Judge You" (Col. 2:16-17)

This warning exposes the danger of the *legalism* of the Gnostic teachers in Colossae. Their doctrines

85

were a strange mixture of Oriental mysticism,
Jewish legalism, and a smattering of philosophy
and Christian teaching. Apparently, the Jewish
legalism played a very important role. This is no
surprise, because human nature thrives in "religious
duties." The flesh is weak when it comes to doing
spiritual things (Matt. 26:41), but it is very strong
when it comes to practicing religious rules and
regulations. Somehow adhering to the religious routine inflates the ego and makes a person content in
his self-righteousness. In discussing this problem,
Paul presented three important truths.

The basis for our freedom (2:16a). It is found
in the word *therefore,* which relates this discussion
to the previous verses. The basis for our freedom
is the Person and work of Jesus Christ. All the
fullness of the Godhead dwells bodily in Him
(2:9). On the cross, He cancelled the debt and the
dominion of the Law (2:14). As believers, we are
under grace as a rule of life and not under Law
(Rom. 6:14ff).

The believing Gentiles in Colossae never were
under the Law of Moses since that law was given
only to Israel (Rom. 9:4). It seems strange that,
now that they were Christians, they would want to
submit themselves to Jewish legalism! Paul had the
same problem with the Gentiles in the churches of
Galatia, and he refuted Jewish legalism in his letter
to the Galatian believers (Gal. 3:1ff). (See the
author's book *Be Free!* [Victor, 1975] for an ex-
pository study of Galatians.)

The person who judges a believer because that
believer is not living under Jewish laws is really
judging Jesus Christ. He is saying that Christ did
not finish the work of salvation on the cross, and
that we must add something to it. He is also saying

that Jesus Christ is not sufficient for all the spiritual needs of the Christian. The false teachers in Colossae were claiming a "deeper spiritual life" for all who would practice the Law. Outwardly, their practices seemed to be spiritual; but in actual fact, these practices accomplished nothing spiritual.

The bondage of legalism (2:16). Let no one tell you otherwise: it *is* bondage! Peter called it a "yoke upon the neck" (Acts 15:10). Paul used the same image when he warned the Galatians: "Stand fast therefore in the liberty wherewith Christ hath made us free, and be not entangled again with the yoke of bondage" (Gal. 5:1).

These legalistic regulations had to do with foods and with eating and drinking (partaking or abstaining). Under the Old Testament system, certain foods were classified as "clean" or "unclean" (see Lev. 11). But Jesus made it clear that, *of itself*, food was neutral. It was what came out of the heart that made a person spiritual or unspiritual (Matt. 15:1-20). Peter was reminded of this lesson again when he was on the housetop in Joppa (Acts 10:9ff) and when he was rebuked in Antioch by Paul (Gal. 2:11ff). "But food does not bring us near to God; we are no worse if we do not eat, and no better if we do" (1 Cor. 8:8, NIV).

It is likely that God's instructions about foods given through Moses had *physical* reasons behind them as well as spiritual. This point that Paul brings up is a different matter. If a man feels he is healthier for abstaining from certain foods, then he should abstain and care for his body. But he should not judge others who can eat that food, nor should he make it a test of spiritual living. Romans 14—15 is the key passage on this subject.

But the legalistic system not only involved diet;

it also involved *days*. Once again, this was bor-
rowed from the laws given through Moses. The Old
Testament Jew was commanded to keep the weekly
Sabbath, which was the seventh day of the week
(Ex. 20:9-11). It is wrong to call Sunday "the
Christian Sabbath" because it is not so designated
in the New Testament. It is "the Lord's Day" (Rev.
1:10), the first day of the week (1 Cor. 16:2; Acts
20:7), the day that commemorates the victorious
resurrection of Jesus Christ from the dead (John
20:1, 19, 26).

The Jews also had their feast days (Lev. 25)
and their special "new-moon" celebrations (see Isa.
1:13). Their religion was tied to the calendar. Now,
all of this had its proper function under the old
dispensation; but it was not meant to be a permanent part of the faith under the new dispensation
(see John 1:17). The Law was a schoolmaster that
helped to train and discipline Israel in the child-
hood of the nation, preparing the people for the
coming of the Messiah. Now that Jesus had come,
the schoolmaster was no longer needed to perform
the same functions (Gal. 3:24—4:11).

Does this mean that the Old Testament Law has
no ministry to New Testament Christians? Of
course not! The Law still reveals the holiness of
God, and in the Law Jesus Christ can be seen
(Luke 24:27). "We know that the Law is good if a
man uses it properly" (1 Tim. 1:8, NIV). The Law
reveals sin and warns of the consequences of sin—
but it has no power to prevent sin or redeem the
sinner. Only grace can do that.

The blessing of grace (2:17). The Law is but a
shadow; but in Christ, we have the reality, the
substance. "The Law is only a shadow of the good
things that are coming" (Heb. 10:1, NIV). Why go

back into shadows when we have the reality in Jesus Christ? This is like trying to hug a shadow when the reality is at hand!

People who religiously observe diets and days give an outward semblance of spirituality, but these practices cannot change their hearts. Legalism is a popular thing because you can "measure" your spiritual life—and even brag about it! But this is a far cry from measuring up to Christ! (Eph. 4:13)

"Let No Man Beguile You of Your Reward" (Col. 2:18-19)

The word translated *beguile* in the King James Version means "to declare unworthy of a prize." It is an athletic term: the umpire disqualifies the contestant because he has not obeyed the rules. The contestant does not cease to be a citizen of the land, but he forfeits the honor of winning a prize. A Christian who fails to obey God's directions does not lose his salvation. But he does lose the approval of the Lord and the rewards He has promised to those who are faithful (1 Cor. 3:8).

It is a gracious act of God that He has promised rewards to those who serve Him. Certainly He does not owe us anything! We ought to be so grateful that He has saved us from judgment that we would serve Him whether or not we received a reward. Most of God's servants probably obey Him out of love and devotion and never think about rewards. Just as there are degrees of punishment in hell (Matt. 23:14), so there will be degrees of glory in heaven—even though all believers will be like Christ in their glorified bodies. The old Puritan Thomas Watson said it perfectly: "Though every vessel of mercy shall be full [in heaven], yet one may hold more than another."

There is, then, the danger that our lives today will rob us of reward and glory tomorrow. The particular peril Paul had in mind here was *mysticism*, the belief that a person can have an immediate experience with the spiritual world, completely apart from the Word of God or the Holy Spirit. The false teachers in Colossae had visions and made contact with angels. In bypassing the Word of God and the Spirit of God, they were opening themselves to all kinds of demonic activity—because Satan knows how to give counterfeit experiences to people (2 Cor. 11:13-15).

The word translated *intruding* was a technical term used by the mystical religions of that day. It meant "to set foot in the inner shrine, to be fully initiated into the mysteries of the religion." No Christian has to go through any initiation ceremony to get into the presence of God. We may have "boldness to enter into the holiest by the blood of Jesus" (Heb. 10:19). We may "come boldly unto the throne of grace" (Heb. 4:16). And as for worshiping angels, *they are our servants!* The angels are "all ministering spirits, sent forth to minister for them who shall be heirs of salvation" (Heb. 1:14).

Of course, all of this mystical ceremony was wrapped up in a false humility that was actually an expression of pride. "I am not good enough to come directly to God," the Gnostic would say, "so I will start with one of the angels."

Trying to reach God the Father through anyone or anything other than His Son, Jesus Christ, is idolatry. Jesus Christ is the one and only Mediator between God and man (1 Tim. 2:5; John 14:6). The person who worships through angels or saints now in heaven does not prove his humility, for he

is not submitting to the authority of God's Word.
Actually, he reveals a subtle kind of pride that
substitutes man-made traditions for the Word of
God. "His unspiritual mind puffs him up with idle
notions" (Col. 2:18, NIV).

True worship always humbles a person. The
mind is awed by the greatness of God; the *heart* is
filled with love for God; and the *will* is submitted
to the purpose God has for the life. The Gnostics,
however, were interested primarily in "deeper
spiritual knowledge," and they ignored God's truth.
Their "inner secrets" gave them a big head, but
not a burning heart or a submissive will. "Knowledge puffs up, but love builds up" (1 Cor. 8:1,
NIV).

It is worth noting that a true spiritual experience
with God leads to submission and service. When
Job met the Lord he said, "I have heard of Thee
by the hearing of the ear, but now mine eye seeth
Thee. Wherefore I abhor myself, and repent in dust
and ashes" (Job 42:5-6). Peter fell down before his
Lord and said, "Depart from me; for I am a sinful
man, O Lord" (Luke 5:8). Isaiah saw the Lord and
confessed how sinful he was (Isa. 6); and when
John saw the risen Christ, he fell at His feet like
a dead man (Rev. 1:17).

The cheap familiarity with which some people
approach God in prayer, or talk about Him in
testimony or conversation, sometimes borders on
blasphemy. The saintly Bishop Westcott of Great
Britain, author of many scholarly commentaries on
various books of the Bible, once wrote: "Every year
makes me tremble at the daring with which people
speak of spiritual things."

Tragically, this "vain religion of the puffed-up
fleshly mind" is but a mere substitute for true

spiritual nourishment from Jesus Christ, the Head of the body, His church. This is one of several passages in the New Testament that pictures the church as the body of Christ. (See Rom. 12:4ff; 1 Cor. 12—14; Eph. 4:4-16; Col. 1:18, 24.) All of us, as believers, are members of the spiritual body, the church, because of the work of the Holy Spirit (1 Cor. 12:12-13). As Christians, we minister to one another in the body just as the various parts of the human body minister to each other (1 Cor. 12:14ff).

But if a believer does not draw on the spiritual nourishment that comes from Christ and other Christians, he becomes weak. The false teachers were not holding to the Head, and therefore they were spiritually undernourished; but *they* thought they were spiritual experts. Imagine thinking yourself a giant when in reality you are a pygmy!

The false teachers were anxious to win converts to their cause; but the spiritual body grows by *nutrition*, not by *addition*. Every member of Christ's body, including the "ligaments and sinews" (joints and bands), is important to the health and growth of the body. No matter what your spiritual gift may be, you are important to the church. In fact, some people who may not have spectacular public ministries are probably just as important behind the scenes as those out in public.

It is through worship, prayer, and the Word that we draw on the spiritual resources of Christ. All of us must be part of a local church where we can exercise our own spiritual gifts (Eph. 4:11-17). "Now to each one the manifestation of the Spirit is given for the common good" (1 Cor. 12:7, NIV). The New Testament says nothing of "isolated saints" outside of the local church.

But it is possible to be *in* a local church and not draw on the Head and the nourishment of the spiritual body. The false teachers in Colossae sought to introduce their teachings into the local assembly; and if they succeeded, they would have caused the spiritual nourishment to *decrease* instead of *increase.* Unless the members of the local assembly abide in Christ, yield to the Spirit, and obey the Word, they cannot experience the life of the Head, Jesus Christ.

There is a fascination with "religious mysticism" that attracts people. Learning mysteries, being initiated into the inner secrets, and having contact with the spirit world all seem exciting.

But these practices are soundly condemned by God. The true Christian glories in Christ, not in his own experience. He follows the Word, led by the Holy Spirit; and as he abides in Christ, he experiences blessing and fruitfulness. He seeks no other experience than that which relates him to the Head, Jesus Christ.

"Let No One Enslave You!" (Col. 2:20-23)

Paul condemned legalism and mysticism; next he attacked and condemned *asceticism.* An ascetic practices rigorous self-denial and even self-mortification in order to become more spiritual. Ascetic practices were popular during the Middle Ages: wearing hair shirts next to the skin, sleeping on hard beds, whipping one's self, not speaking for days (maybe years), going without food or sleep, etc.

There is a definite relationship between legalism and asceticism, for the ascetic often subjects himself to rules and regulations: "touch not, taste not, handle not" (2:21). Certain foods or practices are unholy and must be avoided. Other practices are holy and must never be neglected. The ascetic's entire life is wrapped up in a system of discipline.

As Christians, we admit that physical discipline is needed in our lives. Many of us eat too much and are overweight. Some of us drink too much coffee or cola drinks and are nervous and upset. We believe that our bodies are temples of the Holy Spirit (1 Cor. 6:19-20), yet sometimes we do not care for our bodies as we should. "Physical training is of some value," Paul wrote (1 Tim. 4:8, NIV). Paul disciplined his own body and kept it under control (1 Cor. 9:27). So there is a place in our Christian lives for proper care of our bodies.

But the ascetic hopes to sanctify the soul by his discipline of the body, and it is this heresy that Paul attacked. Just as days and diets have no sanctifying value, neither does fleshly discipline. In this section Paul gave several arguments to prove that the Christian must not engage in religious asceticism.

The Christian's spiritual position (2:20). Asceticism has to do with the rudiments of the world and not the riches of the kingdom. Earlier we saw the word *rudiments* and learned that it meant "the fundamentals or A B Cs of something" (Col. 2:8). In this case, "the rudiments of the world" refer to rules and regulations about foods. As Christians, we are dead to all of this because of our union with Jesus Christ in death, burial, and resurrection (see Col. 2:12-15; Rom. 6). Though we are *in* the world physically, we are not *of* the world spiritually (John 17:15-16). We have been transferred into God's kingdom (Col. 1:13), and therefore we govern our lives by His laws and not the rules of men.

This is not to suggest that Christians are lawless. A student in a Christian school once told me it was "unspiritual" for him to obey the rules! I reminded him that Christians always respect the authority of those over them (1 Peter 2:11ff), and that he knew the rules before he arrived on campus. If he did not like them, he should have stayed home! Paul was not counseling us to be rebels, but he was warning us not to think we are spiritual because we obey certain rules and regulations that pertain to the body.

The futility of ascetic rules (2:21-22). To begin with, these rules did not come from God; they were the inventions of men. God "giveth us richly all things to enjoy" (1 Tim. 6:17). Foods have been "created to be received with thanksgiving" (1 Tim. 4:3). But the "commandments and doctrines" of the false teachers replaced the inspired Word of God (see Mark 7:6-9). The doctrines were what the false teachers believed; the commandments were the regulations they gave in applying their doctrines to practical daily life.

God gave foods to be used, and they "perish with the using" (Col. 2:22). Jesus explained that food went into the stomach, not the heart (Mark 7:18ff). The man who refuses certain foods because they will defile him does not understand what either Jesus or Paul taught: "I know, and am persuaded by the Lord Jesus, that there is nothing unclean of itself" (Rom. 14:14).

Many of us are quick to criticize the ancient monks, the Oriental mystics, and the Hindu or Moslem fakirs; but we fail to see this same error in our own churches. While there are definite connections between physical discipline and health, there is no connection between such discipline and holiness. If we deliberately abstain from some food or drink to keep from hurting a weaker Christian (Rom. 14:13ff), that is one thing. But we must not say that our abstinence makes us more spiritual than another brother who partakes of that food and gives thanks to God (Rom. 14:6).

The deception of asceticism (2:23). The people who practice asceticism have a "reputation" for spirituality, but the product does not live up to the promotion. I am amazed at the way educated people in America flock to see and hear gurus and other Eastern spiritual leaders whose teachings cannot change the human heart. This "self-imposed worship" is not the true worship of God, which must be "in spirit and in truth" (John 4:24). Their humility is false, and their harsh disciplines accomplish nothing for the inner man.

While it is certainly better to exercise self-control than to yield to the physical appetites of the body, we must not think that such self-control is necessarily *spiritually* motivated. The ascetics of many non-Christian religions give evidence of remarkable self-control. The Stoics and their ascetic philosophy were well known in Paul's day. Their adherents could duplicate any discipline that the Gnostic teachers cared to present.

The power of Christ in the life of the believer does more than merely restrain the desires of the flesh: *it puts new desires within him.* Nature determines appetite. The Christian has the very nature of God within (2 Peter 1:4), and this means he has godly ambitions and desires. He does not need *law* on the outside to control his appetites, because he has *life* on the inside! The harsh rules of the ascetics "lack any value in restraining sensual indulgence" (Col. 2:23, NIV). If anything, they eventually bring out the worst instead of the best. In the closing two chapters of this letter, Paul explained how the new life functions in the believer to give him purity and victory.

This section closes the second chapter of Colossians in which the emphasis was on *danger*. Paul defended the preeminence of Jesus Christ, and he refuted the false doctrines of legalism, mysticism, and asceticism. It now remains for us to believe what he wrote and practice these spiritual principles.

The answer to legalism is the spiritual reality we have in Christ. The answer to mysticism is the spiritual union with Christ, the Head of the church. The answer to asceticism is our position in Christ in death, burial, and resurrection.

We put all of this into daily practice as we fellowship with Christ through worship, the Word, and prayer. As we yield to the indwelling Spirit, we receive the power we need for daily living. It is in our fellowship with other believers that we contribute spiritually to the growth of the body, the church, and the other members of the body contribute to us. What a wonderful way to live!

Is Christ preeminent in your life? Are you drawing on His spiritual power, or depending on some man-made "religious" substitute?

8

Heaven
on Earth

Colossians 3:1-11

In the final two chapters of Colossians, Paul moved
into the practical application of the doctrines he
had been teaching. After all, it does little good if
Christians *declare* and *defend* the truth, but fail to
demonstrate it in their lives. There are some Christians who will defend the truth at the drop of a
hat, but their personal lives deny the doctrines
they profess to love. "They profess that they know
God, but in works they deny Him" (Titus 1:16).

We must keep in mind that the pagan religions
of Paul's day said little or nothing about personal
morality. A worshiper could bow before an idol,
put his offering on the altar, and go back to live
the same old life of sin. What a person believed
had no direct relationship with how he behaved,
and no one would condemn a person for his behavior.

But the Christian faith brought a whole new
concept into pagan society: what we believe has a
very definite connection with how we behave! After
all, faith in Christ means being united to Christ;

and if we share His life, we must follow His example. He cannot live in us by His Spirit and permit us to live in sin. Paul connected doctrine with duty in this section by giving his readers three instructions.

Seek the Heavenly (Col. 3:1-4)

The emphasis is on the believer's relationship with Christ.

We died with Christ (3:3a). The fullest explanation of this wonderful truth is found in Romans 6—8. Christ not only died *for* us (substitution), but we died *with* Him (identification). Christ not only died *for* sin, bearing its penalty; but He died *unto* sin, breaking its power. Because we are "in Christ" through the work of the Holy Spirit (1 Cor. 12:13), we died with Christ. This means that we can have victory over the old sin nature that wants to control us. "How shall we, that are dead to sin, live any longer therein?" (Rom. 6:2)

We live in Christ (3:4). Christ is our life. Eternal life is not some heavenly substance that God imparts when we, as sinners, trust the Saviour. Eternal life is Jesus Christ Himself. "He that hath the Son hath life; and he that hath not the Son of God hath not life" (1 John 5:12). We are both dead and alive at the same time—dead to sin and alive in Christ.

Someone has said, "Life is what you are alive to." A child may come alive when you talk about a baseball game or an ice-cream cone. A teenager may come alive when you mention cars or dates. Paul wrote, "For to me to live is Christ" (Phil. 1:21). Christ was Paul's life and he was alive to anything that related to Christ. So should it be with every believer.

Years ago I heard a story about two sisters who enjoyed attending dances and wild parties. Then they were converted and found new life in Christ. They received an invitation to a party and sent their RSVP in these words: "We regret that we cannot attend because we recently died."

We are raised with Christ (3:1). It is possible to be alive and still live in the grave. During World War II, several Jewish refugees hid in a cemetery, and a baby was actually born in one of the graves. However, when Jesus gave us His life, He lifted us out of the grave and set us on the throne in heaven! Christ is seated at the right hand of God, and we are seated there "in Christ."

The word *if* does not suggest that Paul's readers might not have been "risen with Christ," for all of us, as believers, are identified with Christ in death, burial, resurrection, and ascension. The word *since* gives the truer meaning of the word. Our exalted position in Christ is not a hypothetical thing, or a goal to which we strive. It is an accomplished fact.

We are hidden in Christ (3:3). We no longer belong to the world, but to Christ; and the sources of life that we enjoy come only from Him. "Hidden in Christ" means security and satisfaction. The eminent Greek scholar, Dr. A.T. Robertson, comments on this: "So here we are in Christ who is in God, and no burglar, not even Satan himself, can separate us from the love of God in Christ Jesus" (Rom. 8:31-39) (*Paul and the Intellectuals*, Broadman, p. 98).

The Christian life is a "hidden life" as far as the world is concerned, because the world does not know Christ (see 1 John 4:1-6). Our sphere of life is not this earth, but heaven; and the things that attract us and excite us belong to heaven, not to earth. This does not mean that we should ignore our earthly responsibilities. Rather it means that our motives and our strength come from heaven, not earth.

We are glorified in Christ (3:4). Christ is now seated at the Father's right hand, but one day He will come to take His people home (1 Thes. 4:13-18). When He does, we shall enter into eternal glory with Christ. When He is revealed in His glory, we shall also be revealed in glory. According to the Apostle Paul, *we have already been glorified!* (Rom. 8:30) This glory simply has not yet been revealed. Christ has already given us His glory (John 17:22), but the full revelation of the glory awaits the return of the Saviour (Rom. 8:17-25).

Now, in view of our wonderful identification with Christ, we have a great responsibility: "Seek those things which are above" (Col. 3:1). Through Christ's death, burial, resurrection, and ascension, we have been separated from the old life of this world, and we now belong to a new heavenly life.

But how do we "'seek those things which are above"? The secret is found in verse 2: "Habitually set your mind—your attention—on things above, not on things on the earth" (literal translation). Our feet must be on earth, but our minds must be in heaven. This is not to suggest that (as D.L. Moody used to say) we become "so heavenly minded that we are no earthly good." It means that the practical everyday affairs of life get their direction from Christ in heaven. It means further that we look at earth from heaven's point of view.

While attending a convention in Washington, D.C., I watched a Senate committee hearing over television. I believe they were considering a new ambassador to the United Nations. The late Senator Hubert Humphrey was making a comment as I turned on the television set: "You must remember that in politics, how you stand depends on where you sit." He was referring, of course, to the political party seating arrangement in the Senate, but I immediately applied it to my position in Christ. How I stand—and walk—depends on where I sit; *and I am seated with Christ in the heavenlies!*

When the nation of Israel came to the border of the Promised Land, they refused to enter; and, because of their stubborn unbelief, they had to wander in the wilderness for 40 years (see Num. 13—14). That whole generation, starting with the 20-year-olds, died in the wilderness, except for Caleb and Joshua, the only two spies who believed God. How were Caleb and Joshua able to "get the victory" during those 40 difficult years in the wilderness? *Their minds and hearts were in Canaan!* They knew they had an inheritance coming, and they lived in the light of that inheritance.

The Queen of England exercises certain powers and privileges because she sits on the throne. The President of the United States has privileges and powers because he sits behind the desk in the oval office of the White House. The believer is seated on the throne with Christ. We must constantly keep our affection and our attention fixed on the things of heaven, through the Word and prayer, as well as through worship and service. We can enjoy "days of heaven upon the earth" (Deut. 11:21) if we will keep our hearts and minds in the heavenlies.

Slay the Earthly (Col. 3:5-9)
We turn now from the positive to the negative. There are some people who do not like the negative.

"Give us positive doctrines!" they say. "Forget
about negative warnings and admonitions!" But the
negative warnings and commands grow out of the
positive truths of Christian doctrine. This is why
Paul wrote, "Mortify *therefore* . . ."

No amount of positive talk about health will cure
a ruptured appendix. The doctor will have to "get
negative" and take out the appendix. No amount
of lecturing on beauty will produce a garden. The
gardener has to pull weeds! The positive and the
negative go together, and one without the other
leads to imbalance.

The word *mortify* means "put to death." Because
we have died with Christ (v. 3), we have the
spiritual power to slay the earthly, fleshly desires
that want to control us. Paul called this "reckoning"
ourselves to be dead to sin but alive in Christ
(Rom. 6:11). Our Lord used the same idea when
He said, "And if thy right eye offend thee, pluck it
out" (Matt. 5:29-30).

Obviously, neither Paul nor Jesus was talking
about *literal* surgery. Sin does not come from the
eye, hand, or foot; it comes from the heart, the
evil desires within. Centuries ago in England, if a
pickpocket was convicted, his right hand was cut
off. If he was convicted a second time, his left hand
was amputated. One pickpocket lost both hands,
and continued his "trade" by using his teeth!
Physical surgery can never change the heart.

Not only was Paul negative in this paragraph,
but he also *named sins*; and some people do not
like that. These sins belong to the old life and have
no place in our new life in Christ. Furthermore,
God's judgment falls on those who practice these
sins; and God is no respecter of persons. God's
wrath fell on the Gentile world because of these

sins (Rom. 1:18ff), and His wrath will fall again. "Because of these, the wrath of God is coming," Paul warned (Col. 3:6, NIV).

Fornication refers to sexual immorality in general. *Uncleanness* means "lustful impurity that is connected with luxury and loose living." *Inordinate affection* describes a state of mind that excites sexual impurity. The person who cultivates this kind of appetite can always find opportunity to satisfy it. *Evil concupiscence* means "base, evil desires." It is clear that desires lead to deeds, appetites lead to actions. If we would purify our actions, then we must first purify our minds and hearts.

What we desire usually determines what we do. If I create in my children an appetite for candy, then I must satisfy that appetite. If they become overweight and unhealthy, then I must change their appetites, and I must teach them how to enjoy foods other than sweets. "Create in me a clean heart, O God" (Ps. 51:10) should be our prayer; for it is out of the heart that these evil desires come (Mark 7:21-23).

After he had named these sensual sins, Paul added, ". . . and covetousness (which is idolatry)" (Col. 3:5b). *Covetousness* is the sin of always wanting more, whether it be more things or more pleasures. The covetous person is never satisfied with what he has, and he is usually envious of what other people have. This is idolatry, for covetousness puts things in the place of God. "Thou shalt not covet" is the last of the Ten Commandments (Ex. 20:17). Yet this sin can make us break all of the other nine! A covetous person will dishonor God, take God's name in vain, lie, steal, and commit every other sin in order to satisfy his sinful desires.

Do believers in local churches commit such sins? Unfortunately, they sometimes do. Each of the New Testament epistles sent to local churches makes mention of these sins and warns against them. I am reminded of a pastor who preached a series of sermons against the sins of the saints. A member of his congregation challenged him one day and said that it would be better if the pastor preached those messages to the lost. "After all," said the church member, "sin in the life of a Christian is different from sin in the lives of other people."

"Yes" replied the pastor, *"it's worse!"*

After warning us against the sensual sins, Paul then pointed out the dangers of the social sins (Col. 3:8-9). Dr. G. Campbell Morgan called these "the sins in good standing." We are so accustomed to anger, critical attitudes, lying, and coarse humor among believers that we are no longer upset or convicted about these sins. We would be shocked to see a church member commit some sensual sin, but we will watch him lose his temper in a business meeting and call it "righteous indignation."

The picture here is that of a person changing clothes: "put off . . . put on" (vv. 9-10). This relates to the resurrection of Jesus Christ (v. 1); for when He arose from the dead, Jesus Christ left the graveclothes behind (John 20:1-10). He had entered into a glorious resurrection life and had no need for the graveclothes. Likewise, when Lazarus was raised from the dead, Jesus instructed the people to "loose him, and let him go" (John 11:44).

The graveclothes represent the old life with its sinful deeds. Now that we have new life in Christ, we must walk "in newness of life" by putting off the old deeds and desires (Rom. 6:4). We do this by practicing our position in Christ, by reckoning ourselves to be dead to the old and alive to the new.

Paul began with *anger, wrath,* and *malice*—sins of bad attitude toward others. The word *anger* is the same as the word *wrath* (Col. 3:6), referring there to the wrath of God. This word describes habitual attitudes, while *wrath* refers to the sudden outburst of anger. God has a right to be angry at sin and to judge it, because He is holy and just. In fact, there is a righteous anger against sin that ought to characterize the saints (Eph. 4:26). But none of us have the right to "play God" and pass final judgment on others by our attitudes. *Malice* is an attitude of ill will toward a person. If we have malice toward a person, we are sad when he is successful, and we rejoice when he has trouble; this is sinful.

Blasphemy describes speech that slanders others and tears them down. Often among Christians this kind of malicious gossip masquerades as a spiritual concern: "I would never tell you what I know about her, except that I know you'll want to pray about it." Evil speaking is caused by malice (1 Peter 2:1). If you have deep-seated ill will toward a person, you will use every opportunity to say something bad about him.

Filthy communication is just that: foul speech, coarse humor, obscene language. For some reason, some Christians think it is manly or contemporary to use this kind of speech. Low humor sometimes creeps into conversations. If someone says, "Now, take this with a grain of salt!" you can remind him of Colossians 4:6: "Let your speech be always with grace, seasoned with salt." Salt is a symbol of purity, and grace and purity go together.

The final sin Paul named was *lying* (v. 9). He wrote this same warning to the believers in Ephesus (Eph. 4:25). Satan is the liar (John 8:44), while the Holy Spirit is the Spirit of truth (John 14:17; 15:26). When a Christian lies, he is cooperating with Satan; when he speaks the truth in love (Eph. 4:15), he is cooperating with the Spirit of God.

A lie is any misrepresentation of the truth, *even if the words are accurate.* The tone of voice, the look on the face, or a gesture of the hand can alter the meaning of a sentence. So can the motive of the heart. If my watch is wrong and I give a friend the wrong time, that is not a lie. Lying involves the intent to deceive for the purpose of personal gain. An old proverb says, "Half a fact is a whole lie."

Bishop Warren A. Candler was preaching about the lies of Ananias and Sapphira (Acts 5), and asked the congregation, "If God still struck people dead for lying, where would I be?" The congregation snickered a bit, but the smiles disappeared when the Bishop shouted, "I'd be right here—*preaching to an empty church!*"

Strengthen the Christly (Col. 3:10-11)

Because we are alive in Christ, we must seek the things that are above. And, because we died with Christ, we must put off the things that belong to the earthly life of past sin. The result is that we can become like Jesus Christ! God wants to renew us and make us into the image of His Son!

The Greek verbs translated *put off* and *put on* (vv. 9-10) indicate a once-for-all action. When we trust Christ, we put off the old life and put on the new. The old man has been buried, and the new man is now in control. But the verb translated *renewed* is a present participle—"who is constantly being renewed." The *crisis* of salvation leads to the *process* of sanctification, becoming more like Jesus Christ.

The Greeks had two different words for *new*. The word *neos* meant "new in time." We use this word as an English prefix in such words as "neo-orthodoxy" and "neoclassicism." The word *kainos* meant "new in quality, fresh." Sometimes the two words were used interchangeably in the New Testament, but there is still a fundamental difference.

The believer has once and for all put on the "new man" (*neos*), and, as a consequence, he is being renewed (*kainos*). There is a change in quality, for he is becoming like Jesus Christ. The "new Man" is Jesus Christ, the last Adam (1 Cor. 15:45), the Head of the new creation (2 Cor. 5:17).

How does this renewal come about? Through knowledge. The word *knowledge* was one of the key terms in the vocabulary of the Gnostics. But their so-called spiritual knowledge could never change a person's life to make him like Christ. The better he gets to know Christ, the more he becomes like Him (Phil. 3:10).

Man was created in the image of God (Gen. 1:26-27). This involves man's personality (intellect, emotion, will), and man's spirituality (he is more than a body). When man sinned, this image of God was marred and ruined. Adam's children were born in the image of their father (Gen. 5:1, 3). In spite of the ravages of sin, man still bears the image of God (Gen. 9:6; James 3:9).

We were *formed* in God's image, and *deformed* from God's image by sin. But through Jesus Christ, we can be *transformed* into God's image! We must be renewed in the spirit of our minds (Eph. 4:23). As we grow in knowledge of the Word of God, we will be transformed by the Spirit of God to share in the glorious image of God (2 Cor. 3:18). God transforms us by the renewing of our minds (Rom. 12:2), and this involves the study of God's Word. It is the truth that sets us free from the old life (John 8:31-32).

God's purpose for us is that we be "conformed to the image of His Son" (Rom. 8:29). This refers to character, the spiritual quality of the inner man. When we see Jesus Christ, we shall be like Him and have glorified bodies (1 John 3:1-3); but while we are waiting for Him to return, we can become like Him and share His holy image. This is a process of constant renewing as the Spirit of God uses the Word of God.

Human distinctions and differences should be no barrier to holy living in the church. In Jesus Christ, all human distinctions disappear (Col. 3:11). In Christ, there are no nationalities ("neither Greek nor Jew"). There is no recognition of former religious differences ("circumcision nor uncircumcision"). The Gnostics taught that circumcision was important to the spiritual life (Col. 2:11ff). But Paul made it clear that this traditional act of physical surgery gave no advantages in the spiritual life.

There are also no cultural differences in Christ ("barbarian, Scythian"). The Greeks considered all non-Greeks to be barbarians; and the Scythians were the lowest barbarians of all! Yet, in Jesus Christ, a person's cultural status is no advantage or disadvantage. Nor is his economic or political status ("bond or free"). Paul made it clear that a slave should try to get his freedom (1 Cor. 7:20-

23), but he should not think he is handicapped *spiritually* because of his social position.

All of these human distinctions belong to the "old man" and not the "new man." In his letter to the Galatians, Paul added, "There is neither male nor female," and thus erased even differences between the sexes. "Christ is all, and in all," was Paul's conclusion. "For ye are all one in Christ Jesus" (Gal. 3:28).

It is wrong to build the fellowship of the church on anything other than Jesus Christ, His Person and His work. Ministries that are built on human distinctions, such as race, color, or social standing, are not biblical. One of the evidences of spiritual growth and the renewing of the mind is this willingness to receive and love all who sincerely know Christ and seek to glorify Him. The Gnostic "super saints" were trying to isolate the Colossian believers from the rest of the church, and this was wrong. Even though *physically* we do not lose our national heritage when we become Christians, we do not use that heritage as a test of what is spiritual.

"Christ is all and in all" is the emphasis in this letter. "That in all things He might have the preeminence" (Col. 1:18). Because we are complete in Christ, we can look beyond the earthly differences that separate people and enjoy a spiritual unity in the Lord. The Gnostic false teachers, like the false teachers today, tried to rob God's people of the richness of their oneness in Christ. Beware!

We are alive in Christ; therefore, we should seek the heavenly. We are dead in Christ; therefore, we should slay the earthly. We can become like Christ; therefore, we must strengthen the Christly and permit the Spirit to renew our minds, making us more into the image of God.

9

All Dressed Up and Someplace to Go

Colossians 3:12-17

This section completes Paul's exhortation to the Christian to live a holy life. It continues the illustration of *garments*: "Put off . . . put on" (vv. 8-10). He exhorted his readers to put off the grave-clothes of sin and the old life, and to put on the "grace clothes" of holiness and the new life in Christ.

The emphasis in this section is on *motives*. Why should we put off the old deeds and put on the qualities of the new life? Paul explained four motives that ought to encourage us to walk in newness of life (Rom. 6:4).

The Grace of Christ (Col. 3:12-14)

Grace is God's favor to undeserving sinners. Paul reminded the Colossians of what God's grace had done for them.

God chose them (3:12a). The word *elect* means "chosen of God." God's words to Israel through Moses help us to understand the meaning of salvation by grace: "The Lord did not set His love upon

111

you, nor choose you, because ye were more in number than any people; for ye were the fewest of all people. But because the Lord loved you . . . hath the Lord brought you out [of Egypt] with a mighty hand" (Deut. 7:7-8a).

This miracle of divine election did not depend on anything that we are or that we have done; for God chose us in Christ "before the foundation of the world" (Eph. 1:4). If God saved a sinner on the basis of merit or works, nobody would be saved. It is all done through God's grace that it might all bring glory to God.

Of course, *election* is a "sacred secret" that belongs to God's children. It is not a doctrine that we believers explain to the unsaved. "The Lord knows them that are His" (2 Tim. 2:19), so we must leave the working out of His eternal purposes with Him. Our task is to share the good news of the Gospel with a lost world.

God set them apart (3:12). That is the meaning of the word *holy*. Because we have trusted Christ, we have been set apart from the world, unto the Lord. We are not our own; we belong completely to Him (1 Cor. 6:19-20). Just as the marriage ceremony sets apart a man and a woman for each other exclusively, so salvation sets the believer apart exclusively for Jesus Christ. Would it not be a horrible thing, at the end of a wedding, to see the groom run off with the maid of honor? It is just as horrible to contemplate the Christian, living for the world and the flesh.

God loves them (3:12). When an unbeliever sins, he is a creature breaking the laws of the holy Creator and Judge. But when a Christian sins, he is a child of God breaking the loving heart of his Father. Love is the strongest motivating power in the world. As the believer grows in his love for God, he will grow in his desire to obey Him and walk in the newness of life that he has in Christ.

God has forgiven them (3:13). "Having forgiven you all trespasses" (Col. 2:13). God's forgiveness is complete and final; it is not conditional or partial. How is a holy God able to forgive us guilty sinners? Because of the sacrifice of Jesus Christ on the cross. God has forgiven us "for Christ's sake" (Eph. 4:32), and not for our own sake.

Chosen by God, set apart for God, loved by God, and forgiven by God. They all add up to GRACE! Now, because of these gracious blessings, the Christian has some solemn responsibilities before God. He must put on the beautiful graces of the Christian life. Paul named eight graces.

Put on . . . tender mercies (3:12). The Greek uses the term *bowels of compassion,* because the Greek people located the deeper emotions in the intestinal area, while we locate them in the heart. As believers, we need to display tender feelings of compassion toward one another. (See Phil. 2:1ff.) This is not something that we turn on and off, like the TV set. It is a constant attitude of heart that makes us easy to live with.

Put on . . . kindness (3:12). We have been saved because of God's kindness toward us through Jesus Christ (Eph. 2:7; Titus 3:4). We, in turn, ought to show kindness toward others. "Be ye kind one to another" (Eph. 4:32) is God's command.

One of the most beautiful pictures of kindness in the Bible is King David's treatment of the crippled prince, Mephibosheth. (See 2 Samuel 9.) David's desire was to show "the kindness of God" to King Saul's family because of his own love for Saul's son, Jonathan. The young man chosen was

Mephibosheth, Jonathan's son, a poor cripple. If David had acted according to justice, he would have condemned Mephibosheth; for the man belonged to a condemned family. But David acted on the basis of love and grace.

David sought Mephibosheth and assured him not to be afraid. He invited Mephibosheth to live in the palace as a member of his family, and to eat at the king's bountiful table. This is the kindness of God! You and I have experienced an even greater kindness, for as Christians, we are God's children and shall live with Him in heaven forever!

Put on . . . humbleness of mind (3:12). The pagan world of Paul's day did not admire humility. Instead, they admired pride and domination. Jesus Christ is the greatest example of humbleness of mind (Phil. 2:1ff). Humility is not thinking poorly of one's self. Rather, it is having the proper estimate of one's self in the will of God (Rom. 12:3). The person with humbleness of mind thinks of others first and not of himself.

Put on . . . meekness (3:12). Meekness is not weakness; it is power under control. This word was used to describe a soothing wind, a healing medicine, and a colt that had been broken. In each instance, there is *power:* a wind can become a storm; too much medicine can kill; a horse can break loose. But this power is under control. The meek person does not have to fly off the handle because he has everything under control.

Put on . . . long-suffering (3:12). This word is literally "long-temper." The short-tempered person speaks and acts impulsively and lacks self-control. When a person is long-suffering, he can put up with provoking people or circumstances without retaliating. It is good to be able to get angry, for this is a sign of holy character. But it is wrong to get angry quickly at the wrong things and for the wrong reasons.

Put on . . . forbearance (3:13). This word literally means "to hold up" or "to hold back." God is forbearing toward sinners in that He holds back His judgment (Rom. 2:4; 3:25). Meekness, long-suffering, and forbearance go together.

Put on . . . forgiveness (3:13). This is the logical result of all that Paul has written so far in this section. It is not enough that the Christian must endure grief and provocation, and refuse to retaliate; he must also forgive the troublemaker. If he does not, then feelings of malice will develop in the heart; and these can lead to greater sins.

It is Christlike to forgive (Eph. 4:32), and forgiveness opens the heart to the fullness of the love of God. The very instant we have a complaint against another person, we should forgive him in our hearts. ("Family forgiveness" is another matter. We should go to the offender and seek to help him in love. See Matt. 18:15-35.)

Put on . . . love (3:14). This is the most important of the Christian virtues, and it acts like a "girdle" that ties all the other virtues together. All of the spiritual qualities Paul has named are aspects of true Christian love, as a reading of 1 Corinthians 13 will reveal. Love is the first of the fruit of the Spirit and the other virtues follow—joy (v. 16), peace (v. 15), long-suffering, gentleness, kindness, and meekness (v. 12).

When love rules in our lives, it unites all these spiritual virtues so that there is beauty and harmony, indicating spiritual maturity. This harmony and maturity keep the life balanced and growing. The Gnostic system could never do this.

The Peace of Christ (Col. 3:15)

In this verse Paul turned from character to conduct. How can a Christian know when he is doing God's will? One answer is: the peace of Christ in the heart. When the believer loses his inner peace, he knows that he has in some way disobeyed God.

The word translated *rule* is an athletic term. It means "to preside at the games and distribute the prizes." Paul used a variation of this word in his letter to the Colossians: "Let no one declare you unworthy of a prize" (literal translation, Col. 2:18). In the Greek games, there were judges (we would call them *umpires*) who rejected the contestants who were not qualified, and who disqualified those who broke the rules.

The peace of God is the "Umpire" in our believing hearts. When we obey the will of God, we have His peace within; but when we step out of His will (even unintentionally), we lose His peace.

We must beware, however, of a false peace in the heart. Jonah deliberately disobeyed God, yet he was able to go to sleep in the hold of a ship *in a storm!* "I had peace about it!" is not sufficient evidence that we are in the will of God. We must pray, surrender to His will, and seek His guidance in the Scriptures. The peace of heart *alone* is not always the peace of God.

Something else is involved: if we have peace in our hearts, we will be at peace with others in the church. We are called to one body, and our relationship in that body must be one of harmony and peace. If we are out of the will of God, we are certain to bring discord and disharmony to the church. Jonah thought he was at peace, when actually his sins created a storm!

When a Christian loses the peace of God, he

begins to go off in directions that are out of the will of God. He turns to the things of the world and the flesh to compensate for his lack of peace within. He tries to escape, but he cannot escape *himself!* It is only when he confesses his sin, claims God's forgiveness, and does God's will that he experiences God's peace within.

When there is peace in the heart, there will be praise on the lips: ". . . and be ye thankful (Col. 3:15). The Christian out of God's will is never found giving sincere praise to God. When David covered up his sins, he lost his peace and his praise (Ps. 32; 51). When he confessed his sins, then his song returned.

The Word of Christ (Col. 3:16)

This means, of course, the Word of God. The false teachers came to Colossae with man-made traditions, religious rules, and human philosophies. They tried to harmonize God's Word with their teachings, but they could not succeed. God's Word always magnifies Jesus Christ.

It was not the word of false teachers that brought salvation to the Colossians; it was the Word of the truth of the Gospel (Col. 1:5). This same Word gives us life and sustains and strengthens us (1 Peter 1:22—2:3).

The Word will transform our lives if we will but permit it to "dwell" in us richly. The word *dwell* means "to feel at home." If we have experienced the grace and the peace of Christ, then the Word of Christ will feel at home in our hearts. We will discover how rich the Word is with spiritual treasures that give value to our lives.

However, we must not think that Paul wrote this only to individual Christians; for he directed it to the entire church body. "Let the Word of Christ dwell among you" is a possible translation. As it dwells richly in each member of the church, it will dwell richly in the church fellowship.

There is a danger today, as there was in Paul's day, that local churches minimize the Word of God. There seems to be a lack of simple Bible teaching in Sunday School classes and pulpits. Far more interest is shown in movies, musical performances, and various entertainments than in God's Word. Many saved people cannot honestly say that God's Word dwells in their hearts richly, because they do not take time to read, study, and memorize it.

There is (according to Paul) a definite relationship between our knowledge of the Bible and our expression of worship in song. One way we teach and encourage ourselves and others is through the singing of the Word of God. But if we do not know the Bible and understand it, we cannot honestly sing it from our hearts.

Perhaps this "poverty of Scripture" in our churches is one cause of the abundance of unbiblical songs that we have today. A singer has no more right to sing a lie than a preacher has to preach a lie. The great songs of the faith were, for the most part, written by believers who knew the doctrines of the Word of God. Many so-called "Christian songs" today are written by people with little or no knowledge of the Word of God. It is a dangerous thing to separate the praise of God from the Word of God.

Psalms were, of course, the songs taken from the Old Testament. For centuries, the churches in the English-speaking world sang only metrical versions of the Psalms. I am glad to see today a return to the singing of Scripture, especially the

Psalms. Hymns were songs of praise to God written by believers but not taken from the Psalms. The church today has a rich heritage of hymnody which, I fear, is being neglected. Spiritual songs were expressions of Bible truth other than in psalms and hymns. When we sing a hymn, we address the Lord; when we sing a spiritual song, we address each other.

Paul described a local church worship service (Col. 3:16; 1 Cor. 14:26). Note that the believer sings *to himself* as well as to the other believers; and he also sings to the Lord. Our singing must be from our hearts and not just our lips. But if the Word of God is not in our hearts, we cannot sing from our hearts. This shows how important it is to know the Word of God, for it enriches our public and private worship of God.

Our singing must be with grace. This does not mean "singing in a gracious way," but singing because we have God's grace in our hearts. It takes grace to sing when we are in pain, or when circumstances seem to be against us. It certainly took grace for Paul and Silas to sing in that Philippian prison (Acts 16:22-25). Our singing must not be a display of fleshly talent; it must be a demonstration of the grace of God in our hearts.

Someone has said that a successful Christian life involves attention to three books: God's Book, the Bible; the pocketbook; and the hymnbook. I agree. I often use a hymnal in my devotional time, to help express my praise to God. As a believer grows in his knowledge of the Word, he will want to grow in his expression of praise. He will learn to appreciate the great hymns of the church, the Gospel songs, and the spiritual songs that teach spiritual truths. To sing only the elementary songs of the faith is to rob himself of spiritual enrichment.

Before we leave this section, we should notice an important parallel with Ephesians 5:18—6:9. In his letter to the Ephesians, Paul emphasized being filled with the Spirit; in his letter to the Colossians, he emphasized being filled with the Word. *But the evidences of this spiritual fullness are the same!* How can we tell if a believer is filled with the Spirit? He is joyful, thankful, and submissive (Eph. 5:19-21); all of this shows up in his relationships in the home and on the job (Eph. 5:22—6:9). How can we tell if a believer is filled with the Word of God? He is joyful, thankful, and submissive (Col. 3:16—4:1).

The Name of Christ (Col. 3:17)

In modern society, we pay little attention to names. But the ancient world held a man's name to be of utmost importance. Often, during Old Testament days, God changed a person's name because of some important experience or some new development.

As Christians, we bear the name of Christ. The word *Christian* is found only three times in the entire New Testament (Acts 11:26; 26:28; 1 Peter 4:16). The name was given originally as a term of contempt, but gradually it became a name of honor. The name of Christ, then, means *identification*: we belong to Jesus Christ.

But His name also means *authority*. A man's name signed to a check authorizes the withdrawal of money from the bank. The President's name signed to a bill makes it into a law. In the same way, it is in the name of Jesus Christ that we have the authority to pray (John 14:13-14; 16:23-26).

Because Jesus Christ is God, and He has died for us, we have authority in His name.

All that we say and do should be associated with the name of Jesus Christ. By our words and our works, we should glorify His name. If we permit anything into our lives that cannot be associated with the name of Jesus, then we are sinning. We must do and say everything on the authority of His name and for the honor of His name.

Bearing the name of Jesus is a great privilege, but it is also a tremendous responsibility. We suffer persecution because we bear His name (John 15:20-21). I have noticed in conversations that you can tell people you are a Baptist, Presbyterian, Lutheran, or even an atheist, and there will be little response. But if you tell people you are a Christian, and bring the name of Christ into the conversation, almost immediately there is some kind of response, and it is usually negative.

Every parent tries to teach his children to honor the family name. In just a few minutes, a person can disgrace a name that it has taken his ancestors years to build. For example, the Hebrew name *Judah* is a respected name; it means "praise." The New Testament equivalent is "Judas"—and who would name his son Judas?

Note that Paul again mentioned thanksgiving in this Colossian letter. Whatever we do in the name of Christ ought to be joined with thanksgiving. If we cannot give thanks, then we had better not do it or say it! This is the fifth of six references in Colossians to thanksgiving (1:3, 12; 2:7; 3:15, 17; 4:2). When we remember that Paul was a Roman prisoner when he wrote this letter, it makes this emphasis on thanksgiving that much more wonderful.

As we review these four spiritual motivations for Godly living, we are impressed with the centrality of Jesus Christ. We forgive because Christ forgave us (v. 13). It is the peace of Christ that should rule in our hearts (v. 15). The Word of Christ should dwell in us richly (v. 16). The name of Christ should be our identification and our authority. "Christ is all, and in all" (3:11).

Since we are united with Christ through the indwelling Holy Spirit, we have all the resources we need for holy living. But we must be spiritually motivated. Because we have experienced the grace of Christ, we want to live for Him. Because we have enjoyed the peace of Christ, we want to obey Him. We have been enriched by the Word of Christ, and ennobled by the name of Christ; therefore, we want to honor and glorify Him.

Can we desire any higher motivation?

10

A Family
Affair

Colossians 3:18—4:1

Faith in Jesus Christ not only changes individuals;
it also changes homes. In this section, Paul addressed himself to family members: husbands and
wives, children, and household servants. It seems
clear that these persons being addressed were believers since the apostle appealed to all of them
to live to please Jesus Christ.

Something is radically wrong with homes today.
The last report I saw indicated that in America
there are now more broken homes than ever, with
one divorce for every two marriages. Single parent
families are on the increase. Over half of all mothers
are now working outside the home, and many of
them have small children. The average American
child from 6 to 16 watches from 20 to 24 hours of
television each week and is greatly influenced by
what he sees. The "battered child" syndrome continues to increase, with from 2 to 4 million cases
being reported annually, and many not reported
at all.

The first institution God founded on earth was

the home (Gen. 2:18-25; Matt. 19:1-6). As goes
the home, so goes society and the nation. The
breakdown of the home is a sign of the end times
(2 Tim. 3:1-5). Centuries ago Confucius said, "The
strength of a nation is derived from the integrity
of its homes." One of the greatest things we can
do as individuals is help to build godly Christian
homes. Paul addressed the various members of the
family and pointed out the ingredients that make
for a strong and godly home.

Husbands and Wives: Love and Submission (Col. 3:18-19)

Paul did not address the wives first because they
were the neediest! The Gospel radically changed
the position of women in the Roman world. It gave
them a new freedom and stature that some of them
were unable to handle, and for this reason Paul
admonished them. (Similar admonitions are in Eph.
5:18ff and 1 Peter 3:1ff.)

We must not think of *submission* as "slavery" or
"subjugation." The word comes from the military
vocabulary and simply means "to arrange under
rank." The fact that one soldier is a private and
another is a colonel does not mean that one man
is necessarily *better* than the other. It only means
that they have different ranks.

God does all things "decently and in order"
(1 Cor. 14:40). If He did not have a chain of command in society, we would have chaos. The fact
that the woman is to submit to her husband does
not suggest that the man is better than the woman.
It only means that the man has the responsibility
of headship and leadership in the home.

Headship is not dictatorship or lordship. It is

loving leadership. In fact, both the husband and the wife must be submitted to the *Lord* and to *each other* (Eph. 5:21). It is a mutual respect under the Lordship of Jesus Christ.

True spiritual submission is the secret of growth and fulfillment. When a Christian woman is submitted to the Lord and to her own husband, she experiences a release and fulfillment that she can have in no other way. This mutual love and submission creates an atmosphere of growth in the home that enables both the husband and the wife to become all that God wants them to be.

The fact that the Christian wife is "in the Lord" is not an excuse for selfish independence. Just the opposite is true, for her salvation makes it important that she obey the Word and submit to her husband. While it is true that in Jesus Christ "there is neither male nor female" (Gal. 3:28), it is also true that joyful submission is an evidence that the wife belongs to Jesus Christ.

However, the husband has the responsibility of loving his wife; and the word for "love" used here is *agape*—the sacrificing, serving love that Christ shares with His church. A marriage may begin with normal, human, romantic love, but it must grow deeper into the spiritual *agape* love that comes only from God. In the parallel passage (Eph. 5:18ff), Paul made it clear that the husband must love his wife "even as Christ loved the church." Jesus Christ gave His all for the church! He willingly died for us! The measure of a man's love for his wife is not seen only in gifts or words, but in acts of sacrifice and concern for her happiness and welfare.

Paul added a special word of warning for the husbands: "and be not bitter against them" (Col. 3:19). Husbands must be careful not to harbor ill-will toward their wives because of something they did or did not do. A "root of bitterness" in a home can poison the marriage relationship and give Satan a foothold (Heb. 12:15; Eph. 4:31). The Christian husband and wife must be open and honest with each other and not hide their feelings or lie to one another. "Speaking the truth in love" (Eph. 4:15) is a good way to solve family differences. "Let not the sun go down upon your wrath" is a wise policy to follow if you want to have a happy home (Eph. 4:26).

A husband who truly loves his wife will not behave harshly or try to throw his weight around in the home. "Love is patient, love is kind. It does not envy, it does not boast, it is not proud. It is not rude, it is not self-seeking, it is not easily angered, it keeps no record of wrongs" (1 Cor. 13:4-5, NIV).

A wife really has little difficulty submitting to a husband who loves her. She knows he seeks the very best for her, and that he will not do anything to harm her. The husband's love for his wife is seen in his sacrifice for her, and the wife's love for her husband is seen in her submission to him. Where there are sacrifice and submission, in an atmosphere of love, you will find a happy home.

A happy marriage does not come automatically; it is something that must be worked at all the time. As we walk with Christ in submission to Him, we have no problem submitting to one another and seeking to serve one another. But where there is selfishness, there will be conflict and division. If there is bitterness in the heart, there will eventually be trouble in the home.

Where do we get the power to love and to submit? From the Lord. If we are wearing the "grace clothes" described earlier (Col. 3:5-14), and if we have our hearts filled with the peace of Christ and the Word of Christ, then we will contribute to the joy and harmony of the home. If we live to please Christ first, others second, and ourselves last, we will build strong marriages and spiritual homes.

Parents and Children: Encouragement and Obedience (Col. 3:20-21)

There were children in these Christian homes, and Paul addressed part of his letter to them. The normal result of marriage is the bearing of children, and fortunate are those children who are born into Christian homes where there is love and submission. "Be fruitful and multiply" was God's order to our first parents (Gen. 1:28), and this order was given before man sinned. The marriage relationship and the bearing of children are not sinful; rather, they are part of God's mandate to man. In the begetting and bearing of children, the husband and wife share in the creative activity of God.

A great deal is being said about the rights of children, and they *do* have rights. One of them is the right to be born. Another is the right to be born into a dedicated Christian home where they will be raised in the "nurture and admonition of the Lord" (Eph. 6:4). They have the right to have godly parents who will teach them the Word of God and discipline them in love.

John H. Starkey was a violent British criminal. He murdered his own wife, then was convicted for the crime and executed. The officials asked General William Booth, founder of the Salvation Army, to conduct Starkey's funeral. Booth faced as ugly and mean a crowd as he had ever seen in his life, but his first words stopped them and held them: "John

H. Starkey never had a praying mother!"

Children have rights, but they also have responsibilities; and their foremost responsibility is to obey. They are to obey "in all things" and not simply in those things that please themselves. Will their parents ever ask them to do something that is wrong? Not if the parents are submitted to the Lord and to one another, and not if they love each other and their children.

The child who does not learn to obey his parents is not likely to grow up obeying *any* authority. He will defy his teachers, the police, his employers, and anyone else who tries to exercise authority over him. The breakdown in authority in our society reflects the breakdown of authority in the home.

For the most part, children do not *create* problems; they *reveal* them. Parents who cannot discipline themselves cannot discipline their children. If a father and mother are not *under* authority themselves, they cannot *exercise* authority over others. It is only as parents submit to each other and to the Lord that they can exercise properly balanced spiritual and physical authority over their children.

The *measure* of the child's obedience is "all things"; and the *motive* is to please the Lord. It is possible to please the parents and not please the Lord, if the parents are not yielded to the Lord. The family that lives in an atmosphere of love and truth, that reads the Word of God, and that prays together, will have an easier time discovering God's will and pleasing the Lord.

The word *fathers* in verse 21 could be translated "parents," as it is in Hebrews 11:23. Paul made it clear that parents must make it as easy as possible for children to obey. "Provoke not your children"

(Col. 3:21) is a commandment to parents, and how often it is disobeyed! Too often, parents automatically say *no* when their children ask for something, when the parents should listen carefully and evaluate each request. Parents often change their minds and create problems for their children, sometimes by swinging from extreme permissiveness to extreme legalism.

Fathers and mothers should encourage their children, not discourage them. One of the most important things parents can do is spend time with their children. A survey in one town indicated that fathers spent only 37 seconds a day with their small sons! It is an encouragement for children to know that their parents, as busy as they are, take time— *make* time—to be with them.

Parents also need to listen and be patient as their children talk to them. A listening ear and a loving heart always go together. "You took time to have me," a child said to her father, "but you won't take time to listen to me!" What an indictment!

Life is not easy for children, especially Christian children. Their problems might seem small to us, but they are quite large to them! Christian parents must listen carefully, share the feelings and frustrations of their children, pray with them, and seek to encourage them. Home ought to be the happiest and best place in all the world!

Discouraged children are fair prey for Satan and the world. When a child does not get "ego-strength" at home, he will seek it elsewhere. It is a pity that some Christian parents do not help their children develop their personalities, their gifts, and their skills. It is even worse when Christian parents compare one child with another and thereby set up unnecessary competition in the home.

Parents sometimes use their children as weapons for fighting against each other. Father will forbid Junior from doing something, but Mother will veto that order and give her approval. The poor child is caught between his parents, and before long he learns how to play both ends against the middle. The result is moral and spiritual tragedy.

If a home is truly Christian, it is a place of encouragement. In such a home, the child finds refuge from battles, and yet strength to fight the battles and carry the burdens of growing maturity. He finds a loving heart, a watching eye, a listening ear, and a helping hand. He does not want any other place—home meets his needs. In this kind of a home, it is natural for the child to trust Christ and want to live for Him.

Masters and Servants: Honesty and Devotion (Col. 3:22—4:1)

Slavery was an established institution in Paul's day. At least half of the people were slaves. Many of them were well-educated people who carried great responsibilities in the homes of the wealthy. In many homes, the slaves helped to educate and discipline the children.

Why didn't the church of that day openly oppose slavery and seek to destroy it? For one thing, the church was a minority group that had no political power to change an institution that was built into the social order. Paul was careful to instruct Christian slaves to secure their freedom if they could (1 Cor. 7:21); but he did not advocate rebellion or the overthrow of the existing order.

Something should be noted: the purpose of the

early church was to spread the Gospel and win souls, not to get involved in social action. Had the first Christians been branded as an anti-government sect, they would have been greatly hindered in their soul-winning and their church expansion. While it is good and right for Christians to get involved in the promotion of honesty and morality in government and society, this concern must never replace the mandate to go into all the world and preach the Gospel (Mark 16:15).

You will remember that the Book of Colossians was one of three letters that came from Paul's Roman imprisonment; the other two were Ephesians and Philemon. Read Paul's little letter to Philemon and see his attitude toward slavery. Paul did not advise Philemon to treat his runaway slave severely, but to receive him as a brother even though he was still a slave. In fact, Onesimus, the slave, was one of the men who carried this letter to Colossae! (Col. 4:9)

A Christian servant owed complete obedience to his master, as a ministry to the Lord. If a Christian servant had a believing master, that servant was not to take advantage of his master because they were brothers in the Lord. If anything, the servant strived to do a better job because he was a Christian. He showed singleness of heart and gave his full devotion to his master. His work was done heartily, not grudgingly, and as to the Lord and not to men. "Ye serve the Lord Christ" (3:24).

Single hearts and sincere hearts were necessary for Christian servants to please God and serve their masters acceptably. These instructions emphasized the *positive* side of obedience. Servants were to obey to please God, not just to avoid punishment. Even if the master did not commend them, they would have their reward from the Lord. In the same manner, if they disobeyed, the Lord would deal with them even if their master did not. God is no respecter of persons (Acts 10:34; Rom. 2:11; Eph. 6:9; James 2:1, 9).

In our society we do not have slaves. But we can apply these principles to any kind of honest employment. A Christian worker ought to be the best worker on the job. He ought to obey orders and not argue. He ought to serve Christ and not the boss only, and he ought to work whether anybody is watching or not. If he follows these principles, he will receive his reward from Christ even if his earthly master (his boss) does not recognize him or reward him.

I have a friend who, years ago, was fired from his job for working too hard. He was earning money to go to college, and he wanted to give the employer a good day's work each day. The trouble was, his zeal was showing up the laziness of some of the other employees—and they started fighting back. One of them falsely accused my friend of something, and he was fired. He lost his job but he kept his character, and the Lord rewarded him.

In today's complex, competitive world, it is sometimes difficult for a Christian to obey God and hold his job, or get a promotion. But he must obey God just the same and trust Him for what he needs. Unsaved fellow employees may take advantage of the Christian worker, but perhaps this can be an opportunity for the Christian to witness and back up his witness with his life. It is far more important to win a lost soul than to make a few extra dollars.

Just as the husbands and wives and parents and children have mutual and reciprocal responsibilities, so do masters and servants. Paul admonished the Christian masters to treat their servants with fairness and honesty. This would be a new idea to Roman masters, because they considered their slaves as "things," and not people. Masters had almost total control over their slaves and could do with them whatever they pleased. Few unsaved Roman masters ever thought of treating their slaves with fairness, for slaves deserved nothing.

The Gospel did not immediately destroy slavery, but it did gradually change the relationship between slave and master. Social standards and pressures disagreed with Christian ideals, but the Christian master was to practice those ideals just the same. He was to treat his slave like a person and like a brother in Christ (Gal. 3:28). He was not to mistreat him, he was to deal with his slave justly and fairly. After all, the Christian slave was a free man in the Lord, and the master was a slave to Christ (1 Cor. 7:22). In the same way, our social and physical relationships must always be governed by our spiritual relationships.

As we review this very practical section of Colossians, we see once again the preeminence of Jesus Christ in our lives as believers. Christ must be the Head of the home. This series of admonitions is actually a practical application of Colossians 3:17: "And whatsoever ye do in word or deed, do all in the name of the Lord Jesus." It is by His power and authority that we should live in our daily relationships. If He is the preeminent One in our lives, then we will love each other, submit to each other, obey, and treat one another fairly in the Lord.

It would be well for us to review Ephesians 5:18—6:9 and note the parallels between that passage and the one we have just studied. This section of Ephesians emphasizes being filled with the Spirit, while the Letter to the Colossians emphasizes being filled with the Word; but the evidences are the same: joyful, thankful, and submissive living. To be filled with the Spirit means to be controlled by the Word.

The fullness of the Spirit and the fullness of the Word are needed in the home. If family members are controlled by the Spirit of God and the Word of God, they will be joyful, thankful, and submissive—and they will have little trouble getting along with each other. Christian employers and employees will treat each other fairly if they are filled with the Spirit and the Word.

The heart of every problem is the problem of the heart, and only God's Spirit and God's Word can change and control the heart.

Can the people who live with you detect that you are filled with the Spirit and the Word?

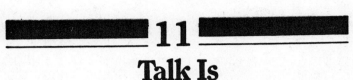

11

Talk Is
NOT Cheap!

Colossians 4:2-9

Never underestimate the power of speech.

A judge says a few words, and a man's life is saved or condemned. A doctor speaks a few words, and a patient either rejoices ecstatically or gives up in despair. Whether the communication is oral or written, there is great power in words. I am told that for every word in Adolph Hitler's book *Mein Kampf*, 125 persons lost their lives in World War II.

The power of speech is a gift from God, and it must be used the way God ordains. In the Book of James, the tongue is compared to a bridle and a rudder, a fire and a poisonous animal, and a fruitful tree and a fountain (James 3). These three pairs of pictures teach us that the tongue has the power to direct, the power to destroy, and the power to delight. The tongue is but a little member in our bodies, but it can accomplish great things for good or for evil.

In this brief section, Paul pointed to four important ministries of speech.

Praying (Col. 4:2-3a)

Prayer and worship are perhaps the highest uses of the gift of speech. Paul was not ashamed to ask his friends to pray for him. Even though he was an apostle, he needed prayer support for himself and his ministry. If a great Christian like Paul felt the need for prayer support, how much more do you and I need this kind of spiritual help! In these few words, Paul described the characteristics of a satisfying and spiritual prayer life.

First, our praying must be *faithful*. "Continue in prayer" (4:2). This means, "Be steadfast in your prayer life; be devoted; don't quit." This is the way the early church prayed (Acts 1:14; 2:46). Too many of us pray only occasionally—when we feel like it or when there is a crisis. "Pray without ceasing" is God's command to us (1 Thes. 5:17). This does not mean that we should walk around muttering prayers under our breath. Rather, it means we should be constantly in fellowship with God so that prayer is as normal to us as breathing.

This is not to suggest that God is reluctant to answer prayer and that we must "wear Him out" by our praying. Quite the opposite is true: God enjoys answering our prayers. But He sometimes delays the answer to increase our faith and devotion and to accomplish His purposes at the right time. God's delays are not always God's denials. As we continue in prayer, our own hearts are prepared for the answer God will give. We find ourselves growing in grace even before His answer comes.

Our praying must also be *watchful*. We must be awake and alert as we pray. The phrase "Watch and pray!" is used often in the Bible. It had its beginning in Bible history when Nehemiah was rebuilding the walls and gates of Jerusalem: "Nevertheless we made our prayer unto our God, and set a watch against them [the enemy] day and night" (Neh. 4:9). Jesus used the phrase (Mark 13:33; 14:38); Paul used it too (Eph. 6:18).

There is no power in dull, listless praying. If there is no fire on the altar, the incense will not rise to God (Ps.141:2). Real praying demands spiritual energy and alertness, and this can come only from the Holy Spirit of God. Routine prayers are unanswered prayers.

Our praying should also be *thankful:* "Watch in the same with thanksgiving (Col. 4:2). Thanksgiving is an important ingredient in successful praying (Phil. 4:6). If all we do is ask, and never thank God for His gifts, we are selfish. Sincere gratitude to God is one of the best ways to put fervor into our praying.

There is always so much to be thankful for! We have already noted the emphasis in Paul's letter to the Colossians on thanksgiving (1:3, 12; 2:7; 3:15, 17; 4:2). When we recall that Paul was a prisoner when he wrote this letter, it makes this emphasis even more wonderful.

Finally, our praying ought to be *purposeful:* "Praying also for us" (4:3). Too often our prayers are vague and general. "Lord, bless the missionaries!" How much better it would be if we would pray for specific needs. By doing so, we would know when God answered and we could praise Him for it. Perhaps it is our lack of faith that causes us to pray generally instead of specifically.

It has well been said that the purpose of prayer is not to get man's will done in heaven, but to get God's will done on earth. Prayer is not telling God what to do or what to give. Prayer is asking God for that which He wants to do and give, according to His will (1 John 5:14-15). As we read the Word and fellowship with our Father, we discover His will and then boldly ask Him to do what He has planned. Richard Trench (1807-1886), archbishop of Dublin, said it perfectly: "Prayer is not overcoming God's reluctance; it is laying hold of His willingness."

Of course, it is possible to pray in our hearts and never use the gift of speech (1 Sam. 1:13); but even then we are using words even if we don't say them audibly. True prayer must first come from the heart, whether the words are spoken or not.

Study Paul's prison prayers (Phil. 1:9-11; Eph. 1:15-23; 3:14-21; Col. 1:9-12) for examples of prayer at its best.

Proclaiming the Word (Col. 4:3b-4)

Paul did not ask for the prison doors to be opened, but that doors of ministry might be opened (1 Cor. 16:9; Acts 14:27). It was more important to Paul that he be a faithful minister than a free man. It is worth noting that in all of Paul's prison prayers, his concern was not for personal safety or material help, but for spiritual character and blessing.

Paul was in prison because of the "mystery of Christ" which related to the Gentiles (see Eph. 3:1-13). The mystery involved God's purpose for the Gentiles in relation to Israel; for in the church, Jews and Gentiles are one (Eph. 2:11-22). Read the account of Paul's arrest in the Jewish temple (Acts 21:18—22:30). Note that the Jews listened to Paul till he spoke the word *Gentiles* (22:21-22). It was Paul's concern for the Gentiles, and his ministry to them that put him into prison.

Even among some believing Jews, there was a

kind of bigotry that wanted to force the Gentiles into a lower position (Acts 15:1ff). This extreme legalistic party wanted the Gentiles to become Jews ceremonially before they could become Christians! Paul and Barnabas met this threat to the Gospel of grace head-on and the council decided in their favor. But the legalistic party continued to oppose Paul and his ministry. They did not want the good news of the mystery of Christ to get to the Gentiles. They wanted to maintain their air of Jewish superiority.

How strange that Paul would want God to help him do the very thing that had caused his arrest! He had no intention of giving up his ministry or of changing his message. When John Bunyan was arrested for preaching illegally and put into prison, he was told that he would be released if he promised to stop preaching. "If I am out of prison today," he replied, "I will preach the Gospel again tomorrow, by the help of God."

How could Paul share the mystery of Christ when he was a prisoner? Paul's case was discussed by many people; Paul was also able to witness to the guards to whom he was chained (Phil. 1:12-18). Imagine being chained to the Apostle Paul! Through this witness, the Gospel was carried into parts of Rome that would have been inaccessible to Paul had he been a free man. There were even "saints in Caesar's household"! (Phil. 4:22)

The proclamation of the Gospel is empowered by prayer. The Spirit of God uses the Word of God as we come to the throne of grace and ask God for His blessing. We must never separate the Word of God from prayer, because God has joined them together (Acts 6:4).

A visitor at Spurgeon's Tabernacle in London

was being shown around the building by the pastor, Charles Spurgeon.

"Would you like to see the powerhouse of this ministry?" Spurgeon asked, as he showed the man into a lower auditorium. "It is here that we get our power, for while I am preaching upstairs, hundreds of my people are in this room praying." Is it any wonder that God blessed Spurgeon's preaching of the Word?

You, as a church member, can assist your pastor in the preaching of the Word by praying for him. Never say to your pastor, "Well, the least I can do is to pray for you." The *most* you can do is to pray! Pray for your pastor as he prepares the Word, studies, and meditates. Pray that the Holy Spirit will give deeper insights into the truths of the Word. Pray too that your pastor will practice the Word that he preaches so that it will be real in his own life. As he preaches the message, pray that the Spirit will give him freedom of utterance, and that the Word will reach into hearts and minds in a powerful way. (It wouldn't hurt to pray for other church leaders too.)

The proclaiming of the Word of God is a great privilege and a tremendous responsibility. You do not have to be an ordained preacher or a missionary to share God's Word. Even in your daily conversation you can drop the seed of the Word into hearts, and then pray that God will water that seed and bring forth fruit.

Witnessing to the Lost (Col. 4:5-6)

"Them that are without" refers to those who are outside the family of God. Jesus made a distinction between His disciples and those who were outside (Mark 4:11). Paul also made this same distinction

(1 Cor. 5:12-13). Those of us who are born again are the "spiritual insiders" because we belong to God's family and share His life.

However, as Christians, we must never have a sanctified superiority complex. We have a responsibility to witness to the lost around us and to seek to bring them into God's family. To begin with, we have the responsibility to *walk wisely* (Col. 4:5). *Walk* refers, of course, to our conduct in daily life. The unsaved outsiders watch us Christians and are very critical of us. There must be nothing in our lives that would jeopardize our testimony.

This story has often been told about Dr. Will H. Houghton, who pastored the Calvary Baptist Church in New York City and later served as president of Chicago's Moody Bible Institute till his death in 1946. When Dr. Houghton became pastor of the Baptist Tabernacle in Atlanta, a man in that city hired a private detective to follow Dr. Houghton and report on his conduct. After a few weeks, the detective was able to report to the man that Dr. Houghton's life matched his preaching. As a result, that man became a Christian.

What does it mean to "walk in wisdom"? For one thing, it means that we are careful not to say or do anything that would make it difficult to share the Gospel. It also means we must be alert to use the opportunities God gives us for personal witnessing. "Redeeming the time" means buying up the opportunity (Eph. 5:16). This is a commercial term and pictures the Christian as a faithful steward who knows an opportunity when he sees one. Just as a merchant seizes a bargain when he finds one, so a Christian seizes the opportunity to win a soul to Christ.

Walking in wisdom also includes doing our work, paying our bills, and keeping our promises. We must "walk honestly toward them that are without" (1 Thes. 4:12). A friend of mine went into a store to make a purchase for his church. The salesman asked, "Is _____ a member of your church?" My friend said that he was, and the salesman proceeded to tell him how much money that church member owed his store and how difficult it was to get anything from him. It would probably have been futile for my friend to have witnessed to that clerk.

Christians in general and Christian leaders in particular, must have "a good report of them which are without" (1 Tim. 3:7). When members of a church are calling a new pastor, they ought to investigate his testimony among his neighbors and the businessmen who know him. Even though unsaved people are in the dark spiritually (2 Cor. 4:3-4), they have a great deal of discernment when it comes to the things of this life (Luke 16:8). It is unfortunate when members of a church call a pastor who has not paid his bills and has left behind a bad witness to unsaved people.

It is not enough simply to walk wisely and carefully before unbelievers. We must also *talk* with them and share the Gospel message with them. But we must take care that our speech is controlled by *grace,* so that it points to Christ and glorifies the Lord. This means we must have grace in our hearts (Col. 3:16), because it is from the heart that the mouth speaks. With grace in our hearts and on our lips, we will be faithful witnesses and not judges or prosecuting attorneys!

The Lord Jesus Christ spoke with grace on His lips. "And all . . . wondered at the gracious words

which proceeded out of His mouth" (Luke 4:22).
Among the many statements about Jesus Christ in
Psalm 45 (a messianic psalm) is this: "Grace is
poured into Thy lips" (v. 2). Even when our Lord
was dealing with sin, He spoke words of grace.

Our speech is supposed to "minister grace unto
the hearers" (Eph. 4:29). But it cannot do that
unless we have grace in our hearts and in our
words. "Speaking the truth in love" (Eph. 4:15)
is God's ideal for our conversation.

Why did Paul add, "seasoned with salt"? (Col.
4:6) In that day, salt was used as a preservative as
well as a seasoner. We should never say to anyone,
"Now, take this with a grain of salt." *We* must
put the salt into our speech to make sure it is pure
and properly seasoned. "Let no corrupt communication proceed out of your mouth" (Eph. 4:29).
Our speech must be pure.

Salt was also added to the sacrifices (Lev. 2:13).
Perhaps Paul was suggesting that we look on our
words as sacrifices offered to God, just as our words
of praise are spiritual sacrifices (Heb. 13:15). It
would no doubt help us to say the right things in
the right manner if we remembered that our words
are looked on as sacrifices to God.

It is unfortunate when a Christian speaks in a
rude or coarse manner, particularly when the unsaved are listening. "Be ready always to give an
answer to every man that asketh you a reason of
the hope that is in you with meekness and fear"
(1 Peter 3:15). Meekness is the opposite of harsh-
ness, and fear is the opposite of arrogance. There
is no place in a Christian's conversation for a
know-it-all attitude. While we need to have con-
·victions and not compromise, we must also culti-
vate a gracious spirit of love.

The Christian's *walk* and *talk* must be in harmony with each other. Nothing will silence the lips like a careless life. When character, conduct, and conversation are all working together, it makes for a powerful witness.

Sharing Burdens (Col. 4:7-9)

Paul did not spell out the details of his personal situation in this letter. He left it to his two spiritual brothers, Tychicus and Onesimus, to share the burdens with the church in Colossae. This is another wonderful ministry of speech: we can share our needs and burdens with others; then they can encourage and assist us.

When Paul left Ephesus, he was accompanied by seven other believers—among them, Tychicus (Acts 20:4). These men were helping Paul deliver the love offering from the Gentile churches to the poor saints in Judea (1 Cor. 16:1; 2 Cor. 8—9). It is possible that Tychicus and Trophimus were the two brethren Paul referred to in his second letter to the Corinthians (see 2 Cor. 8:19-24).

Tychicus shared Paul's Roman imprisonment and no doubt was helpful to him in many ways. Paul chose Tychicus and Onesimus to deliver the Ephesian letter (Eph. 6:21) and the Colossian letter (Col. 4:7-9). Of course, they also took the personal letter to Philemon. Paul instructed Tychicus to share with the Colossian Christians all the details of his situation there in Rome.

Paul's description of Tychicus reveals what a splendid Christian Tychicus really was. He was a *beloved brother*, willing to stay with Paul even though the situation was difficult. How encouraging it is to have a Christian at your side when everything seems to be against you!

Tychicus was also a *faithful minister*. His love revealed itself in action. He ministered *to* Paul, and he also ministered *for* Paul to assist him in his many obligations. Someone has said that the greatest ability in the world is dependability, and this is true. Paul could depend on Tychicus to get the job done.

Tychicus was also Paul's *fellow servant*. Though he was not an apostle himself, he was assisting Paul in his apostolic ministry. Paul and Tychicus worked together in the service of the Lord. Later, Paul was able to send Tychicus to Crete (Titus 3:12), and then to Ephesus (2 Tim. 4:12).

It was not easy for Tychicus to be associated with Paul, the prisoner; for Paul had many enemies. Nor was it easy for Tychicus to travel as he did, assisting Paul in his various tasks. Tychicus did not take the easy way, but rather the right way. Our churches today could use more members like Tychicus!

Paul also mentioned Onesimus ("one of you") who himself came from Colossae. He was the runaway slave who belonged to Philemon and who had been won to Christ through Paul's ministry in Rome. Paul sent Onesimus back to his master with a letter asking Philemon to receive him and forgive him. It is interesting to note that Paul also called Onesimus *faithful* and *beloved*. Onesimus had been a believer only a short time, and yet he had already proved himself to Paul.

These two men had a dual ministry to perform: to encourage the Colossian Christians, and to inform them about Paul's situation. Is it wrong for God's people to share information in this way? Of course not! Paul was not begging for money or asking for sympathy. He wanted the Colossian saints to know his situation so they could pray for him. While it is true that some Christian workers "use" circumstances selfishly to enlist support, this was not true of Paul. He simply wanted his friends in Colossae to know the facts and to support him in prayer.

In our home, we receive a number of missionary prayer letters. We read them and try to note the special burdens and needs. In my own private devotions, I use several prayer calendars that help me remember to pray about specific needs for different ministries. I appreciate knowing the facts so that I can intercede in a specific way. I also enjoy getting reports of how God has answered prayer, for this encourages my faith.

Praying, proclaiming the Word, witnessing, and sharing burdens—these are four wonderful ministries of speech. How much better it is to be involved in these ministries than to be using our tongues for gossip, malicious criticism, and other sinful purposes.

Let's make David's prayer our prayer: "Set a watch, O Lord, before my mouth; keep the door of my lips" (Ps. 141:3)

12

Friends,
Romans,
Countrymen

Colossians 4·10-18

Paul was not only a soul-winner; he was a great friend-maker. If my count is correct, there are more than 100 different Christians (named and unnamed) associated with Paul in the Book of Acts and in his epistles. He named 26 different friends in Romans 16 alone!

It was customary in Paul's day to close each letter with personal greetings. Friends did not see one another that much, and letter service was very slow and limited. Of course, Paul's greetings were much more than social; they conveyed his genuine spiritual concern for his friends. In this closing section, Paul sent personal greetings to Colossae from six of his associates in the ministry: Aristarchus, John Mark, and Jesus Justus, all of whom were Jews; and Epaphras, Luke, and Demas, who were Gentiles. Paul then added special greetings to two church assemblies, with a special word to one of the pastors.

When we first read this list of names, we are probably not greatly moved. But when we get behind the scenes and discover the drama of these men's lives as they worked with Paul, the list becomes very exciting. We can categorize these men into three groups.

The Men Who Stayed (Col. 4:10-11, 14a)

This group is made up of three Jews (Aristarchus, John Mark, Jesus Justus), and one Gentile (Luke). All of them were characterized by faithfulness to the Apostle Paul in his hour of special need. They were the men who stayed.

Aristarchus (Col. 4:10a) was identified as Paul's fellow prisoner, and also as Paul's fellow worker (v. 11). Aristarchus was from Macedonia and was one of Paul's traveling companions (Acts 19:29). He was originally from Thessalonica (Acts 20:4) and willingly risked his life in that Ephesian riot (Acts 19:28-41). He sailed with Paul to Rome (Acts 27:2), which meant he also experienced the storm and shipwreck that Luke so graphically described in Acts 27.

Aristarchus stayed with Paul no matter what the circumstances were—a riot in Ephesus, a voyage, a storm, or even a prison. It is not likely that Aristarchus was an official Roman prisoner. "Fellow prisoner" probably means that Aristarchus shared Paul's confinement with him so that he could be a help and comfort to the apostle. He was a voluntary prisoner for the sake of Jesus Christ and the Gospel.

Paul could not have accomplished all that he did apart from the assistance of his friends. Aristarchus stands out as one of the greatest of Paul's helpers. He did not look for an easy task. He did not run when the going got tough. He suffered with Paul and labored with Paul.

John Mark (Col. 4:10b), the writer of the second Gospel, played a very important part in the early history of the church. He too was a Jew, a native of Jerusalem where his mother, Mary, kept "open house" for the believers (Acts 12:12). John Mark was a cousin of Barnabas, the man who went with Paul on that first missionary journey (Acts 13:1-3). It is a good possibility that John Mark was led to faith in Christ through the ministry of Peter (1 Peter 5:13).

When Paul and Barnabas set out on that first missionary journey, they took John Mark with them as their assistant. He probably took care of the travel arrangements, supplies, etc. But when the going got tough, John Mark abandoned the preachers and returned home to Jerusalem (Acts 13:5-13).

Why John quit is not explained in Scripture. Perhaps he was afraid, for the group was about to move into dangerous territory. Perhaps he resented the fact that Paul was taking over the leadership of the mission and replacing his relative, Barnabas. Or, maybe John Mark resented Paul's ministry to the Gentiles. Whatever the reason or excuse, he left them and returned home.

Later, when Paul and Barnabas wanted to go on a second journey, Paul refused to take John Mark along (Acts 15:36-41). Was Paul wrong in his assessment of this young man? Perhaps, but we cannot blame Paul for being cautious when John Mark had failed him in the past. Paul was not running a popular tour; he was seeking to win lost souls to Christ. No amount of danger or inconvenience could hinder Paul from reaching unbelievers with

the Gospel. It was too bad that John Mark caused
a division between Paul and Barnabas. However,
we must admit that Paul did forgive John Mark
and commend him: "Take Mark and bring him
with thee: for he is profitable to me for the ministry" (2 Tim. 4:11).

Mark, Titus, and Timothy were young men who
served as special representatives for the Apostle
Paul. He could send them to churches that were
having problems and trust them to help solve them.
By the grace of God, John Mark had overcome his
first failure and had become a valuable servant of
God. He was even chosen to write the Gospel of
Mark!

John Mark is an encouragement to everyone who
has failed in his first attempts to serve God. He
did not sit around and sulk. He got back into the
ministry and proved himself faithful to the Lord
and to the Apostle Paul. He was one of the men
who stayed.

I might add that it is good to be a Barnabas and
encourage younger Christians in the Lord. Perhaps
John Mark would have made it without the help of
cousin Barnabas, but I doubt it. God used Barnabas
to encourage John Mark and restore him to service
again. Barnabas lived up to his name: "son of encouragement" (Acts 4:36, NIV).

Jesus Justus (Col. 4:11) was a Jewish believer
who served with Paul, but we know nothing about
him. The name *Jesus* (Joshua) was a popular
Jewish name, and it was not unusual for Jewish
people to have a Roman name as well (Justus).
John Mark is a case in point. Jesus Justus repre-
sents those faithful believers who serve God but
whose deeds are not announced for the whole
world to know. He was a fellow worker with Paul

and a comfort to Paul, and that is all we know about him. However, the Lord has kept a faithful record of this man's life and ministry and will reward him accordingly.

Luke (Col. 4:14a) was a very important man in the early church. He was a Gentile, yet he was chosen by God to write the Gospel of Luke and the Book of Acts. He is probably the only Gentile writer of any book of the Bible. He was also a physician, and was dearly loved by Paul. The profession of medicine had been perfected by the Greeks, and physicians were held in the highest regard. Even though Paul had the power to heal people, he traveled with a physician!

Luke joined Paul and his party at Troas (note the pronoun *we* in Acts 16:10). Luke traveled with Paul to Jerusalem (Acts 20:5ff) and was with him on the voyage to Rome (Acts 27:1ff). No doubt Luke's personal presence and his professional skill were a great encouragement to Paul during that very difficult time. While God can and does bring strength and healing in miraculous ways, He also uses the means provided in nature, such as medication. When my wife and I ministered to missionaries in Africa, a physician friend and his wife traveled with us; and we were grateful for their help.

Luke remained with Paul to the very end (see 2 Tim. 4:11). God used Luke to write the Book of Acts and to give us the inspired history of the early church and the ministry of Paul. Luke is a glowing example of the professional man who uses his skills in the service of the Lord and gives himself to go wherever God sends. He was a beloved Christian, a skillful physician, a devoted friend, and a careful historian—all wrapped up in one!

The Man Who Prayed (Col. 4:12-13)

We met Epaphras at the beginning of this study, for he was the man who founded the church in Colossae (Col. 1:7-8). He had been led to Christ through Paul's ministry in Ephesus, and had returned home to share the good news of salvation. It seems likely that Epaphras also founded the churches in Laodicea and Hierapolis (v. 13). In our modern terms, Epaphras became a "home missionary."

What motivated Epaphras to share the Gospel? He was "a servant of Christ" (v. 12). Paul called him "our dear fellow servant . . . a faithful minister of Christ" (1:7). Epaphras loved Jesus Christ and wanted to serve Him and share His message of salvation. But he did not do it alone. Epaphras also believed in the ministry of the local church, and in working with other saints. He was not just a "servant"; he was a *fellow* servant."

I was chatting one day with a foreign mission executive about a mutual friend who had been forced to resign from his work on the field. "There was no problem with sin or anything like that," my friend explained. "His whole difficulty is that he is a loner. He can't work well with other people. On the mission field, it's a team effort or it's nothing."

One of the secrets of the ministry of Epaphras was his prayer life. Paul knew about this because Epaphras and Paul shared the same room, and when Epaphras prayed, Paul knew about it. What were the characteristics of this man's prayer life?

He prayed constantly (v. 12—"always"). He was a good example of Paul's admonition: "Continue in prayer" (Col. 4:2). Epaphras did not pray only when he felt like it, as do many Christians today.

Nor did he pray when he was told to pray, or when the other believers prayed. He was constantly in prayer, seeking God's blessing.

He prayed fervently (v. 12—"laboring fervently"). The word used here means "agonizing." It is the same word used for our Lord's praying in the Garden (Luke 22:44). We get the impression that prayer was serious business with Epaphras! This Greek word was used to describe the athletes as they gave themselves fully to their sports. If church members today put as much concern and enthusiasm into their praying as they did into their baseball games or bowling, we would have revival!

He prayed personally (v. 12—"for you"). Epaphras did not pray around the world for everybody in general and nobody in particular. He centered his intercession on the saints in Colossae, Laodicea, and Hierapolis. No doubt he mentioned some of them by name. Prayer for Epaphras was not an impersonal religious exercise, for he carried these people in his heart and prayed for them personally.

He prayed definitely. If you had asked Epaphras, "What are you praying for?" he could have told you. His great desire was that the believers in those three assemblies might mature in their Christian faith. Paul used four significant words to summarize the prayer of Epaphras, and these four words also summarize the message of the Book of Colossians: "perfect—complete—all—will."

Epaphras was concerned that these Christians know and do the will of God. But he wanted them to be involved in *all* the will of God, not just in part of it. (*All* is a key word in Colossians, used over 30 times.) He also wanted them to stand *perfect* and *complete* in God's will. The Gnostic teachers offered these Christians "perfection and maturity," but they could not deliver the goods. Only in Jesus Christ can we have these blessings. "And ye are complete in Him," for only in Christ does the fullness of God dwell (Col. 2:9-10).

This request carries the thought of being mature and perfectly assured in the will of God, and parallels Paul's prayer burden (Col. 2:2). "Full assurance in the will of God" is a tremendous blessing! It is not necessary for the believer to drift in life. He can know God's will and enjoy it. As he learns God's will and lives it, he matures in the faith and experiences God's fullness.

He prayed sacrificially (v. 13—"great zeal" or "much distress"). Real prayer is difficult. When Jesus prayed in the Garden, He sweat great drops of blood. Paul had "great conflict" (agony) as he prayed for the Colossians (2:1), and Epaphras also experienced "much distress." This does not mean that we must wrestle with God in order to get Him to answer. But it does mean that we must throw ourselves into our praying with zeal and concern. If there is no burden, there can be no blessing. To rephrase what John H. Jowett said about preaching: "Praying that costs nothing, accomplishes nothing."

All of the men with Paul were named and commended in one way or another, but Epaphras was the only one commended for his prayer ministry. This does not mean that the other men did not pray; but it does suggest that prayer was his major interest and ministry. Epaphras was Paul's fellow prisoner (Phile. 23)—but even confinement could not keep him from entering the courts of heaven and praying for his brothers and sisters in the churches.

E.M. Bounds was a prayer warrior of the last generation. He would often rise early in the morning and pray for many hours before he began the work of the day. His many books on prayer testify to the fact that Bounds, like Epaphras, knew how to agonize in prayer before God. (If you have never read *Power in Prayer* [Baker] by E.M. Bounds, by all means do so.)

I am impressed with the fact that Epaphras prayed for believers in three different cities. We are fortunate today if church members pray for their own pastor and church, let alone believers in other places! Perhaps one reason that revival tarries is because we do not pray fervently for one another.

The Man Who Strayed (Col. 4:14b)

Demas is mentioned only three times in Paul's letters, and these three references tell a sad story. First he is called "Demas . . . my fellow laborer" and is linked with three good men—Mark, Aristarchus, and Luke (Phile. 24). Then he is simply called "Demas," and there is no special word of identification or commendation (Col. 4:14). But the third reference tells what became of Demas: "For Demas hath forsaken me, having loved this present world" (2 Tim. 4:10).

At one point in his life, John Mark had forsaken Paul; but he was reclaimed and restored. Demas forsook Paul and apparently was never reclaimed. His sin was that he loved this present world. The word *world* refers to the whole system of things that runs this world, or "society without God." In the first of his epistles, John the Apostle pointed out that the world entices the believer with "the lust of the flesh, the lust of the eyes, and the pride of life" (1 John 2:15-17). Which of these traps caught Demas, we do not know; perhaps he fell into all three.

But we do know that Christians today can succumb to the world just as Demas did. How easy it is to maintain a religious veneer, while all the time we are living for the things of this world. Demas thought that he could serve two masters, but eventually he had to make a decision; unfortunately, he made the wrong decision.

It must have hurt Paul greatly when Demas forsook him. It also hurt the work of the Lord, for there never has been a time when the laborers were many. This decision hurt Demas most of all, for he wasted his life in that which could never last. "He that doeth the will of God abideth forever" (1 John 2:17).

After conveying greetings from his friends and fellow servants, Paul himself sent greetings to the sister churches in Laodicea and Hierapolis. These people had never seen Paul (Col. 2:1), yet he was interested in them and concerned about their spiritual welfare.

We know nothing about Nymphas, except that he had a church meeting in his house. (Some versions read *Nympha* and seem to indicate that this believer was a woman.) In the first centuries of the church, local assemblies met in private homes. Even today, many new local churches get their starts this way. It was not until the Christian faith emerged from persecution into official government approval that church buildings were constructed. It really matters little where the assembly meets, so long as Jesus Christ is the center of the fellowship. (For other examples of "the church in the home," see Rom. 16:5 and 1 Cor. 16:19.)

Paul's great concern was that the Word of God be read and studied in these churches. The verb *read* means "to read aloud." There would not be copies of these letters for each member. It is a strong conviction of mine that we need to return to the public reading of the Word of God in many of our churches. "Give attendance to reading" (1 Tim. 4:13) means the public reading of God's Word.

It is worth noting that the various letters from Paul were good for *all* of these assemblies. In my ministry, I have shared God's Word in many different places and situations, and it has always reached the heart and met the need. Even in different cultures, God's Word has a message for the heart. God's Word does not have to be edited or changed to meet different problems in various situations, for it is always applicable.

What was "the epistle from Laodicea"? We do not know for sure. Some scholars think that the Epistle to the Ephesians was this missing letter, but this idea is pure speculation. The fact that this letter has been lost does not mean we are missing a part of God's inspired Word. Some of Paul's correspondence with the church at Corinth has also been lost. God not only inspired His Word, but He providentially watched over it so that nothing would be lost that was supposed to be in that Word. Instead of wondering about what we do not have, we should be applying ourselves to what we do have!

When we compare Colossians 4:17 with Philemon 2, we get the impression that Archippus belonged to the family of Philemon. Possibly, he was Philemon's son and the pastor of the church that met in Philemon's house. We cannot prove this, of course, but it does seem a logical conclusion. This would make Apphia the wife of Philemon.

Paul's last words before his salutation are directed at Archippus as an encouragement to continue faithfully in his ministry. Was Archippus discouraged? Had the Gnostic false teachers invaded his church and created problems for him? We do not know. But we do know that pastors of local churches face many problems and carry many burdens, and they often need a word of encouragement.

Paul reminded Archippus that his ministry was a gift from God, and that he was a steward of God who would one day have to give an account of his work. Since the Lord gave him his ministry, the Lord could also help him carry it out in the right way. Ministry is not something we do for God; it is something God does in and through us.

The word *fulfill* carries with it the idea that God has definite purposes for His servants to accomplish. He works in us and through us to complete those good works that He has prepared for us (see Eph. 2:10). Of course, *fulfill* also parallels the theme of Colossians—the fullness of Jesus Christ available to each believer. We are able to fulfill our ministries because we have been "filled full" through Jesus Christ.

Unless we make a practical application of Bible doctrine, our study is in vain. After reading this letter and studying it, we cannot help but see that we have in Jesus Christ all that we can ever want or need. All of God's fullness is in Jesus Christ and we have been made complete in Him. What an encouragement this must have been to Archippus! What an encouragement it should be to us today!

Paul usually dictated his letters to a secretary (see Rom. 16:22) and then signed his name at the end. He always added a sentence about the grace of God, for this was his "trademark" (see 2 Thes. 3:17-18). The combination of his signature and "grace" gave proof that the letter was authentic.

The New Testament contains many references to Paul's bonds and the fact that he was a prisoner. (See Acts 20:23; 23:18, 29; 26:29; Phil. 1:7, 13-14, 16; 2 Tim. 1:8; 2:9; Phile. 10, 13; Eph. 3:1; 4:1.) Why did Paul want them to remember his bonds? Primarily because those bonds were a reminder of his love for lost souls, especially the Gentiles. He was "the prisoner of Jesus Christ for you Gentiles" (Eph. 3:1). Paul's bonds were evidence of his obedience to the Lord and his willingness to pay any price so that the Gentiles might hear the Gospel.

Even today, there are devoted Christians who are in bonds because of their faithfulness to the Lord. We ought to remember them and pray for them. "Remember them that are in bonds, as bound with them" (Heb. 13:3).

As we come to the close of our study of this remarkable letter, we must remind ourselves that we are complete in Jesus Christ. We should beware of any teaching that claims to give us "something more" than we already have in Christ. All of God's fullness is in Him, and He has perfectly equipped us for the life that God wants us to live. We do not live and grow by *addition*, but by *appropriation*.

May the Lord help us to live as those who are complete in Christ.

Victor Books by Warren Wiersbe

Be Alert (2 Peter, 2 & 3 John, Jude). Sharpen your spiritual discernment as Dr. Wiersbe uncovers the disguises of today's religious imposters—6-2380

Be Complete (Colossians). A study showing how false teachers infiltrated the Colossian church. In this book, the author reminds readers of the preeminence of Christ and of their completeness in Him—6-2726

Be Confident (Hebrews). You can remain unshaken in a shaking society, confident that God is shaking things so you might learn to live by faith—6-2728

Be Encouraged (2 Corinthians). God can turn your trials into triumphs and your sufferings into service—6-2620

Be Faithful (1 & 2 Timothy, Titus). How to be faithful to the Word, your tasks, people who need you—6-2732

Be Free (Galatians). A challenge for you to live in the true freedom you have in Jesus Christ—6-2733

Be Hopeful (1 Peter). We can expect to suffer for our faith, but we can be hopeful. God's grace is ours for the asking!—6-2737

Be Joyful (Philippians). Here are four things that can rob you of joy, and how to overcome them—6-2739

Be Loyal (Matthew). This 26-chapter study examines the life of Christ the King: the miracle of His birth, the compassion of His ministry, and His victory over death—6-2313

Be Mature (James). Learn how you can overcome problems by attaining spiritual maturity—6-2754

Be Ready (1 & 2 Thessalonians). Examine the implications of the doctrine of the Second Coming and the need to get ready for the event—6-2773

Be Real (1 John). Discover the character of true love as revealed in Jesus Christ, with pertinent illustrations that apply truth to life—6-2774

Be Rich (Ephesians). Learn how you can find untold wealth and riches from God—6-2775

Be Right (Romans). A clear and practical exposition of Romans, rich in doctrine and applications for today—6-2778

Be Wise (1 Corinthians). See what a difference it makes when you follow God's wisdom instead of man's knowledge—6-2304

Meet Yourself in the Psalms. From selected psalms, Dr. Wiersbe shows that God gives us new vision and strength to turn tragedy into triumph—6-2740

Windows on the Parables. Look through the parables as a mirror to view our inner selves and an open window to glimpse God—6-2710